Valentine : Coloring book

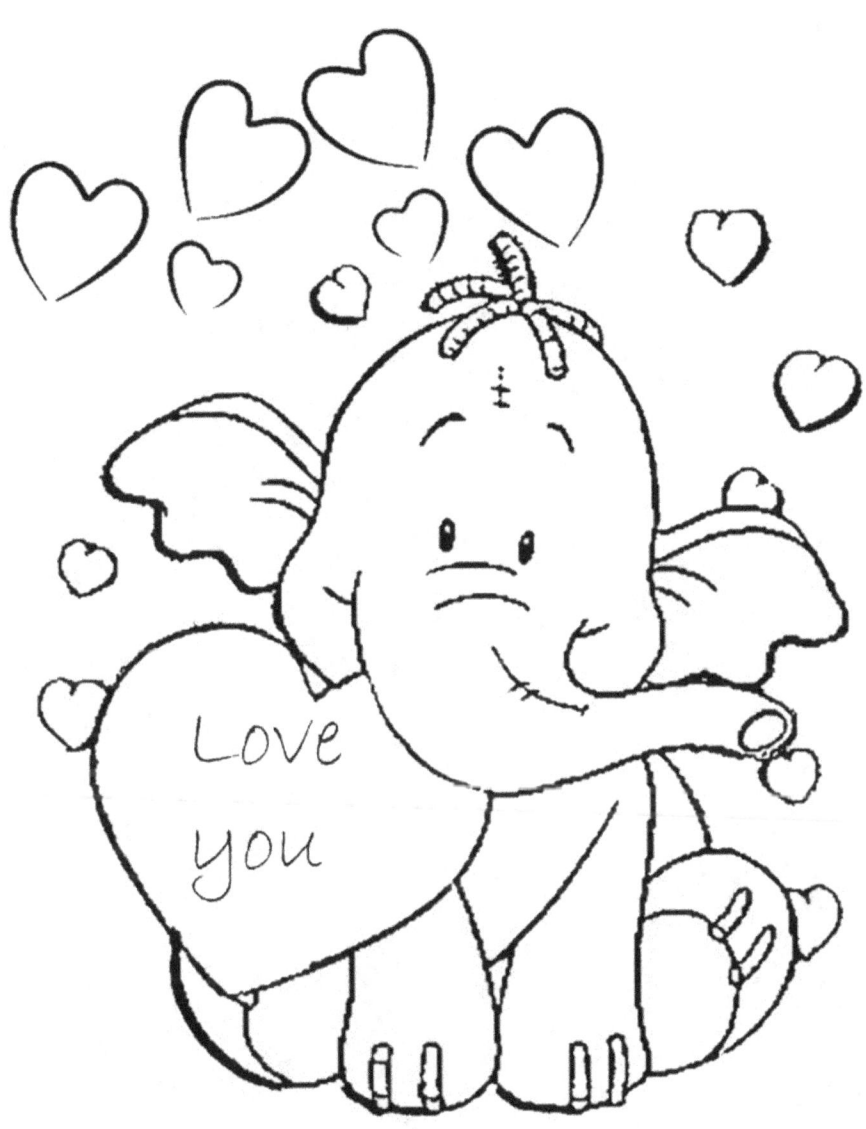

Nina Packer

Magic Valentine: Coloring book
For Kids and teens

Copyright: Published in the United States by Nina Packer
Published December 2017

ISBN-13: 978-1981794713

ISBN-10: 1981794719

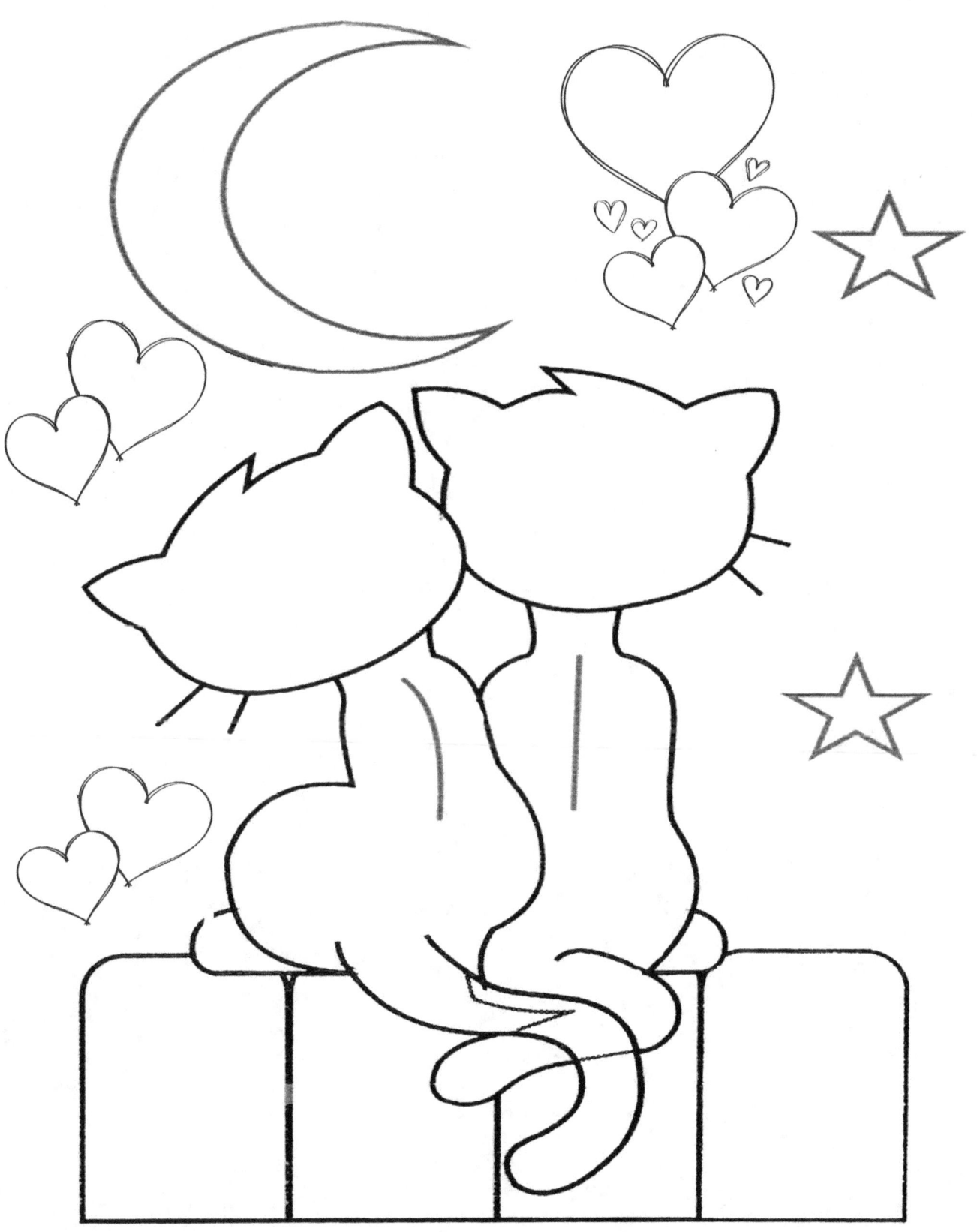

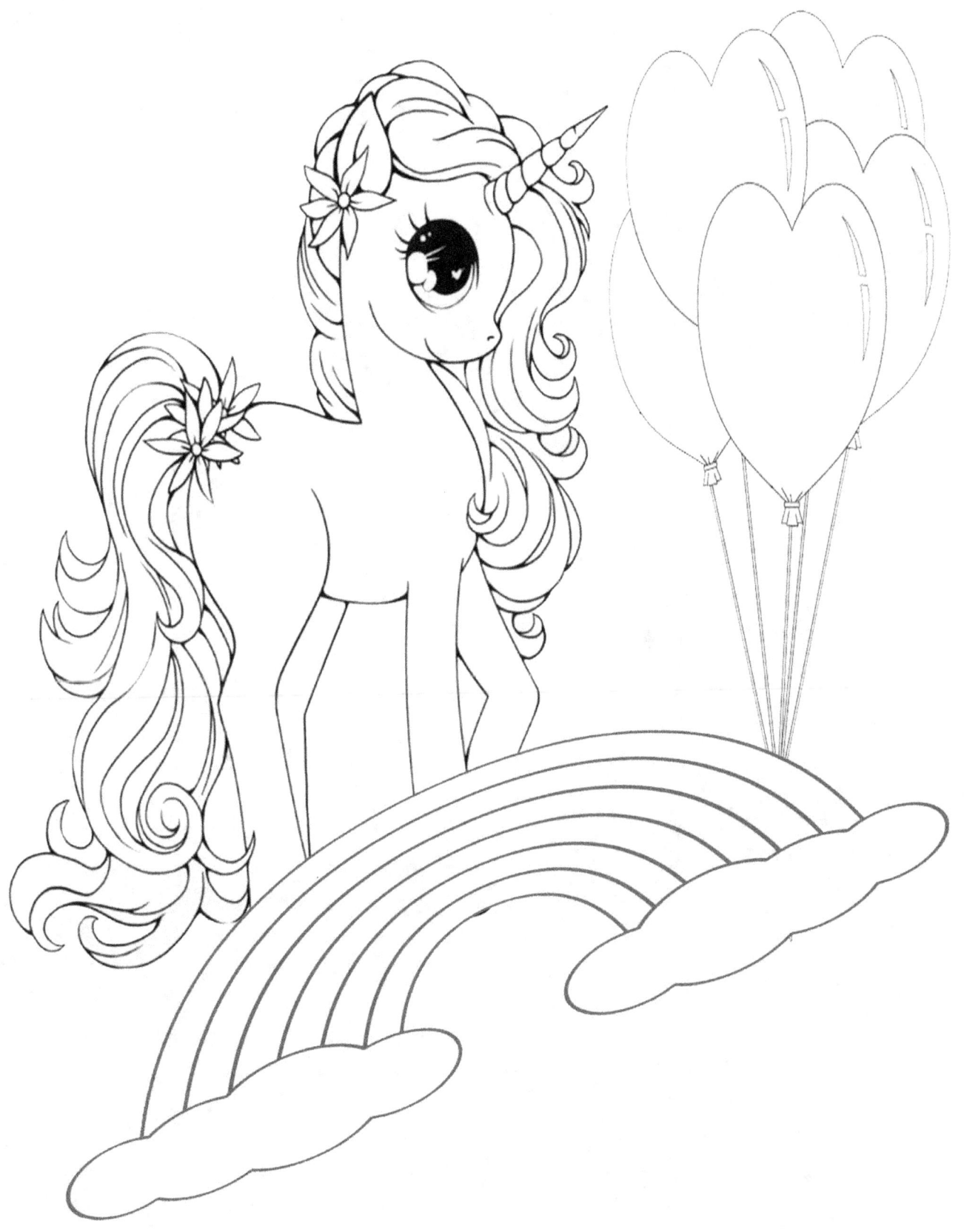

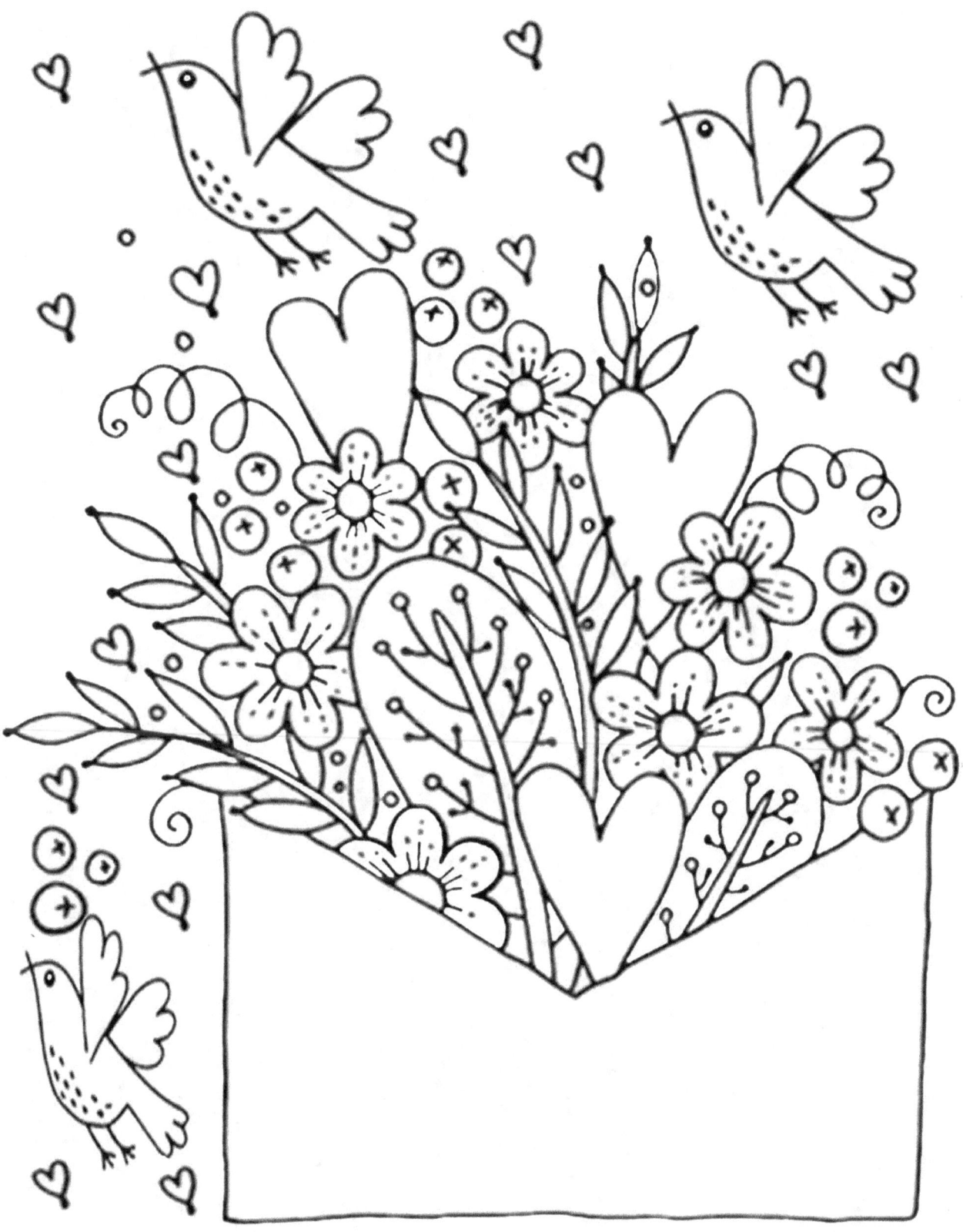

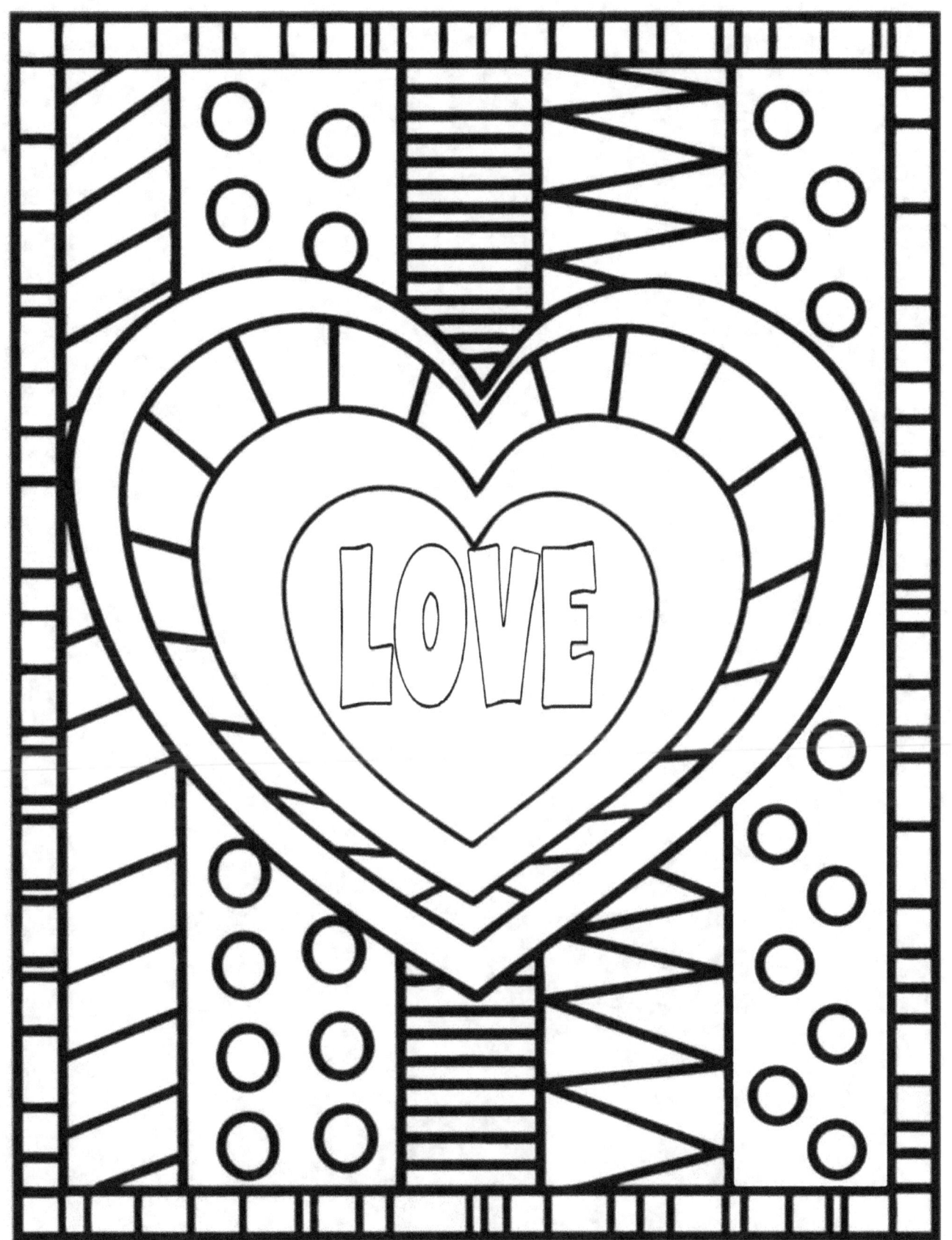

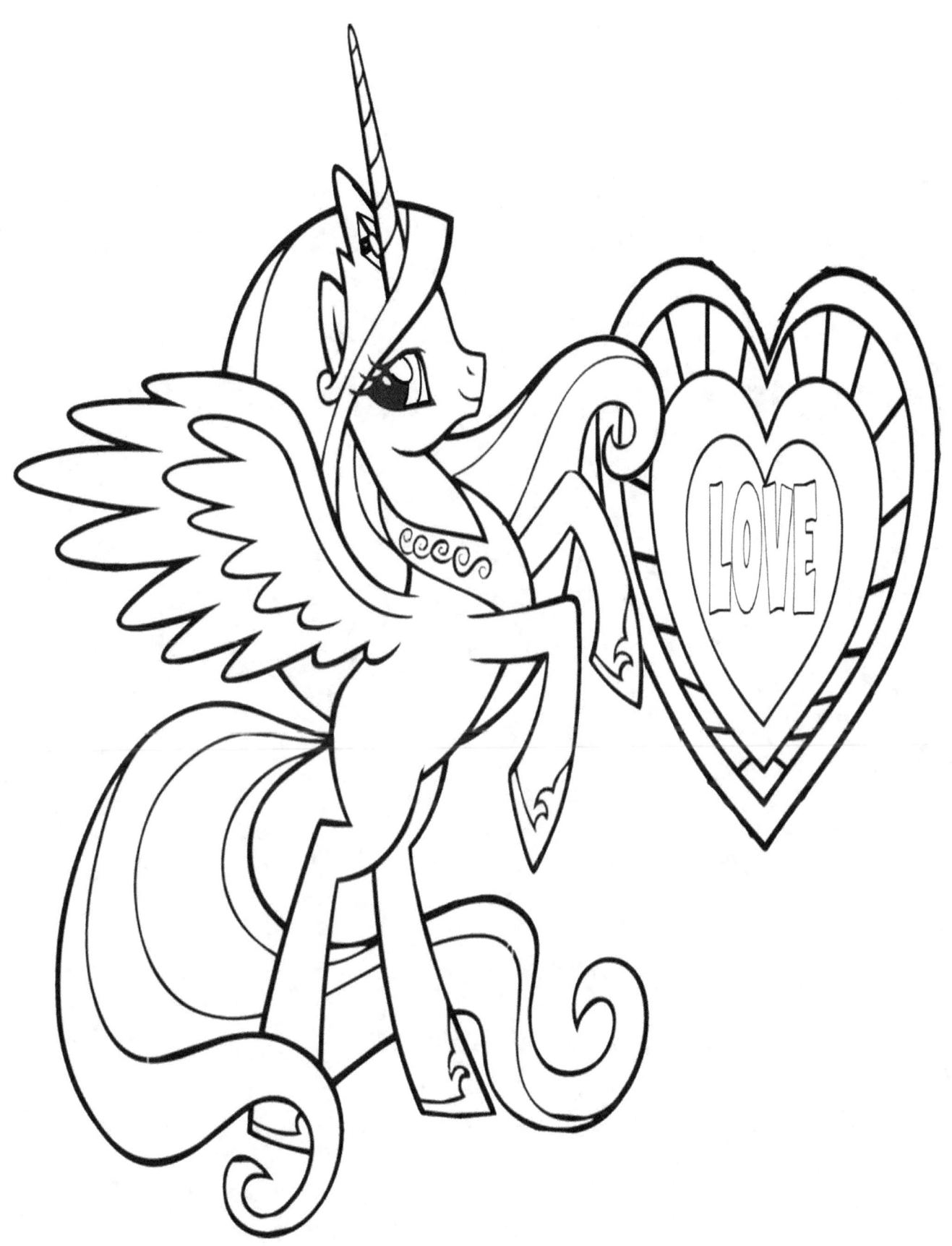

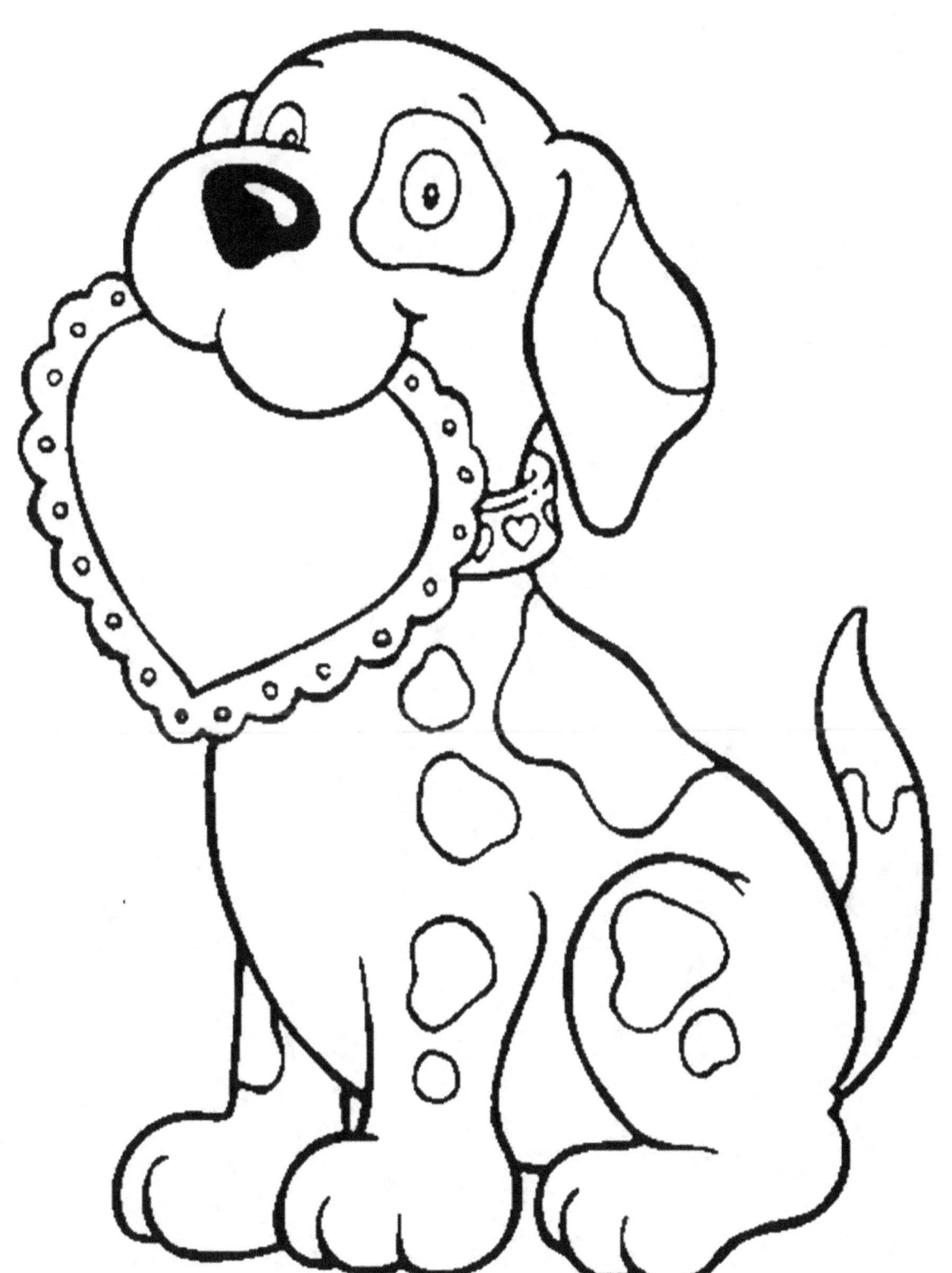

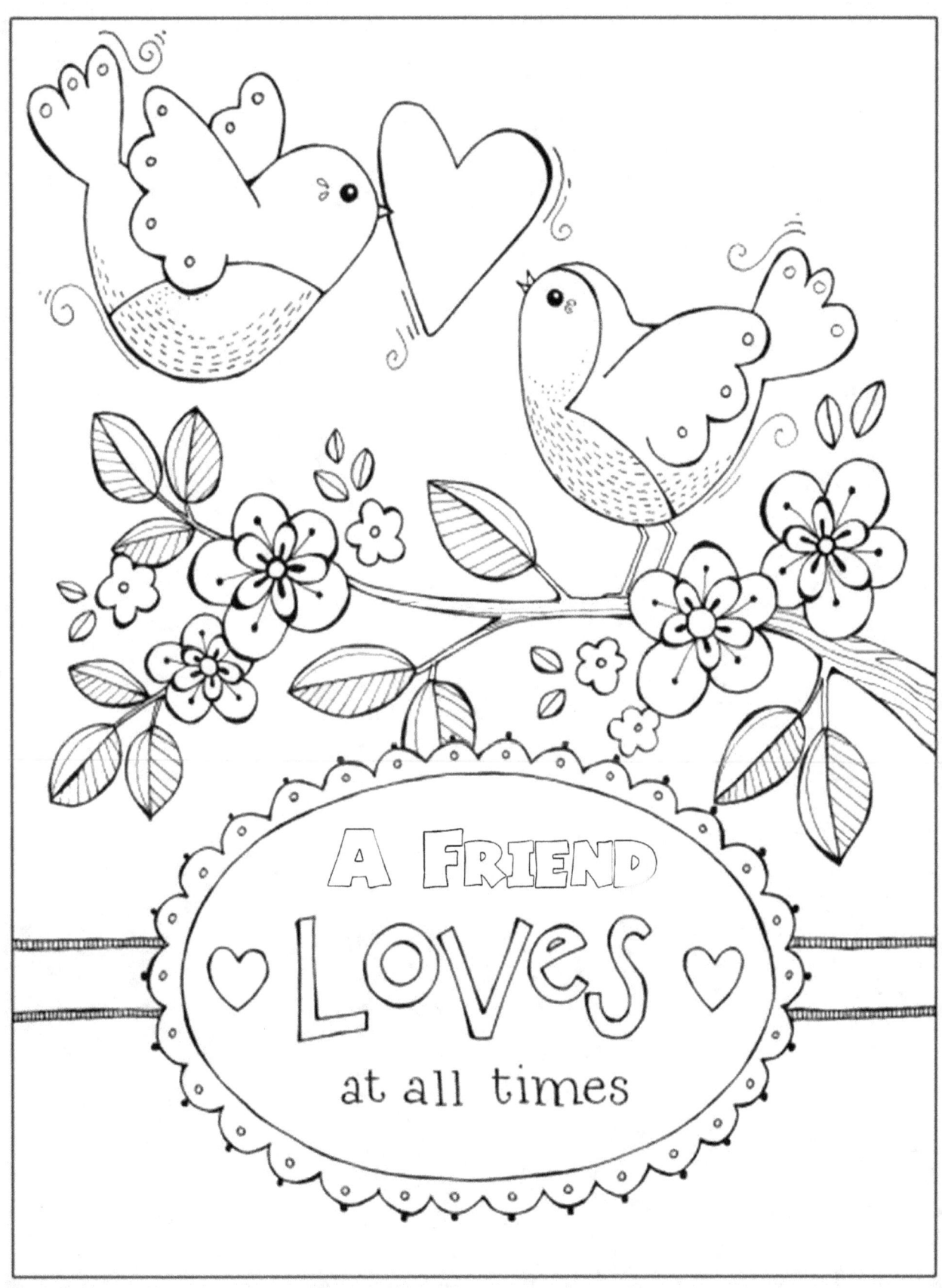

A Friend Loves at all times

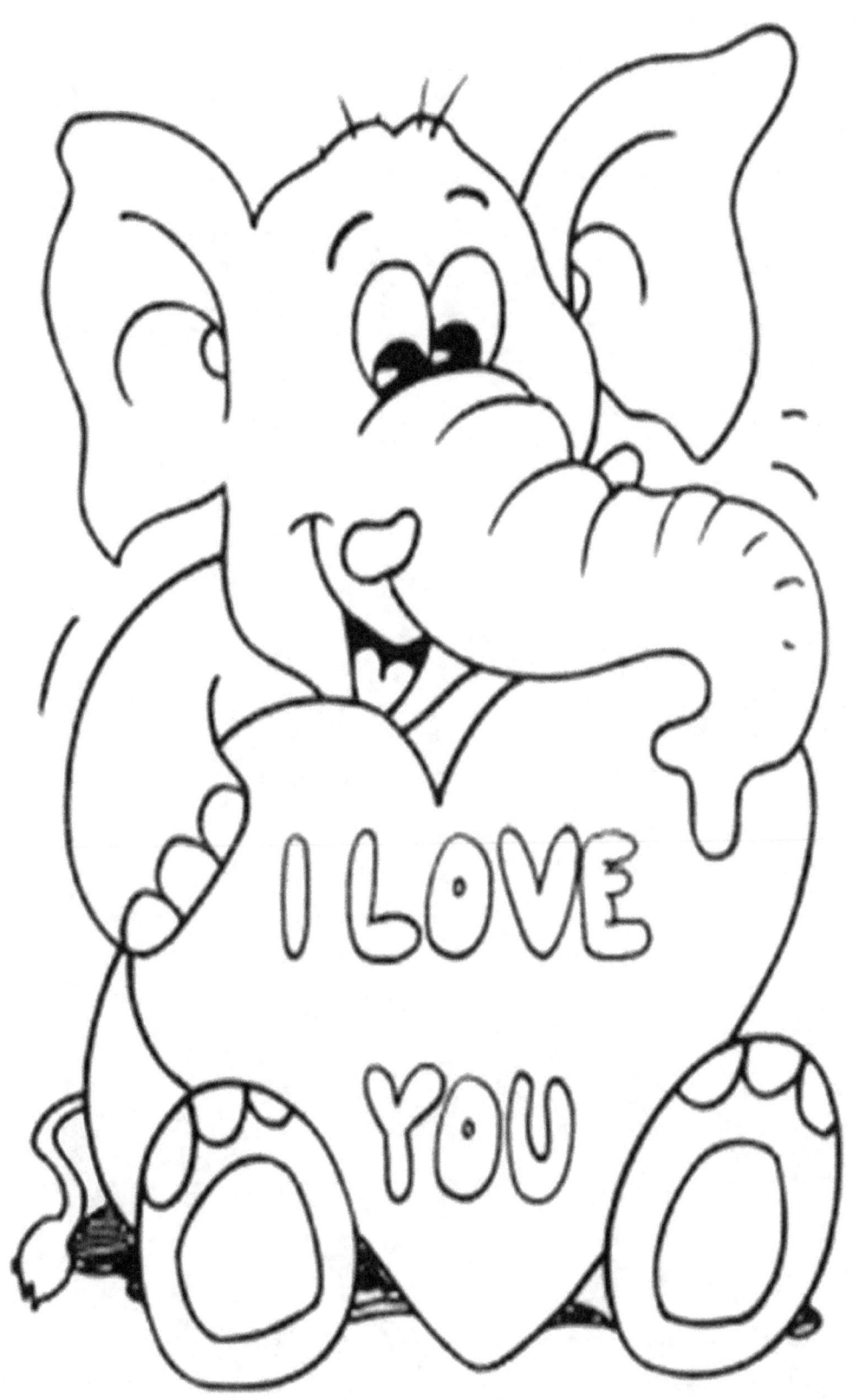

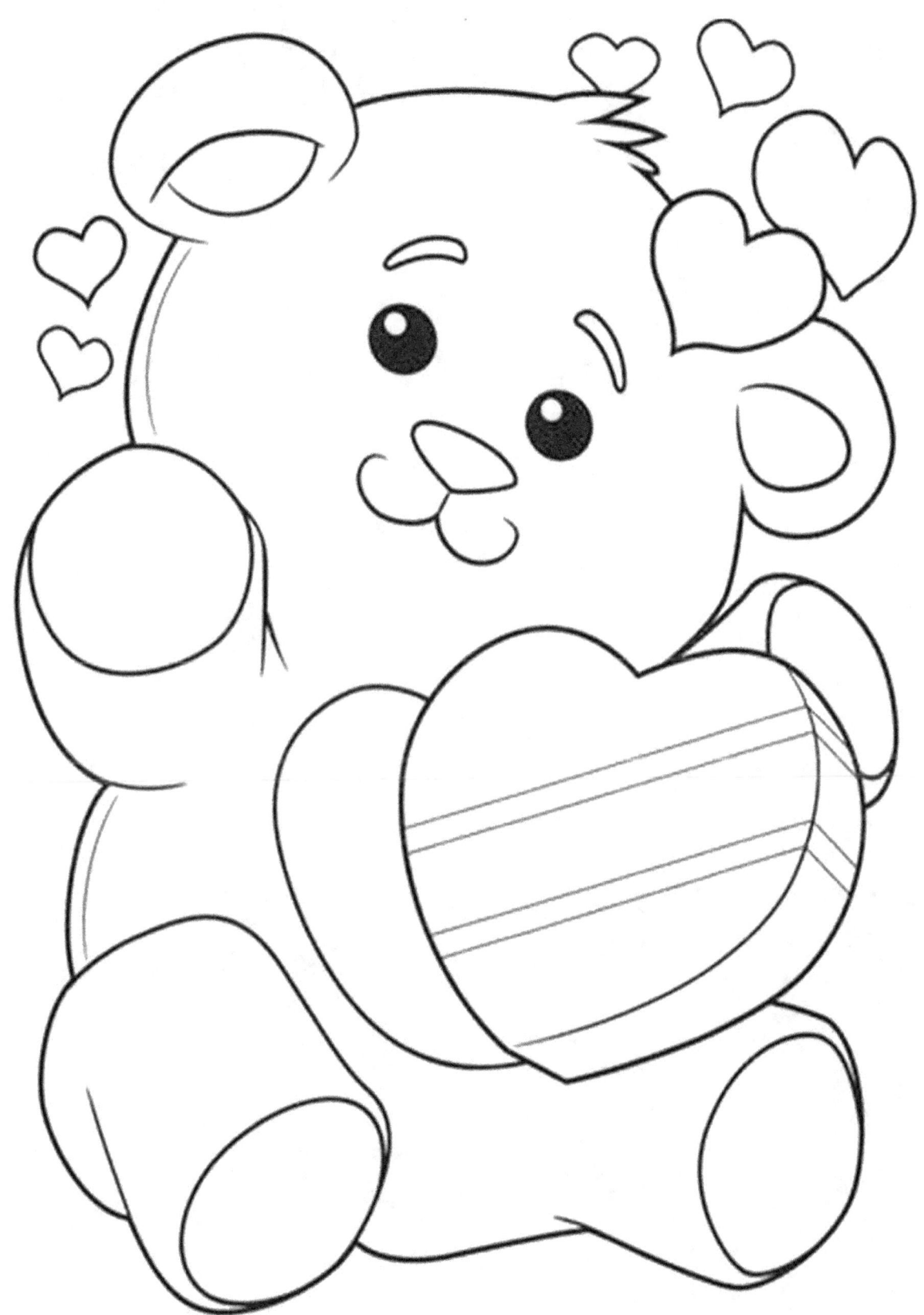

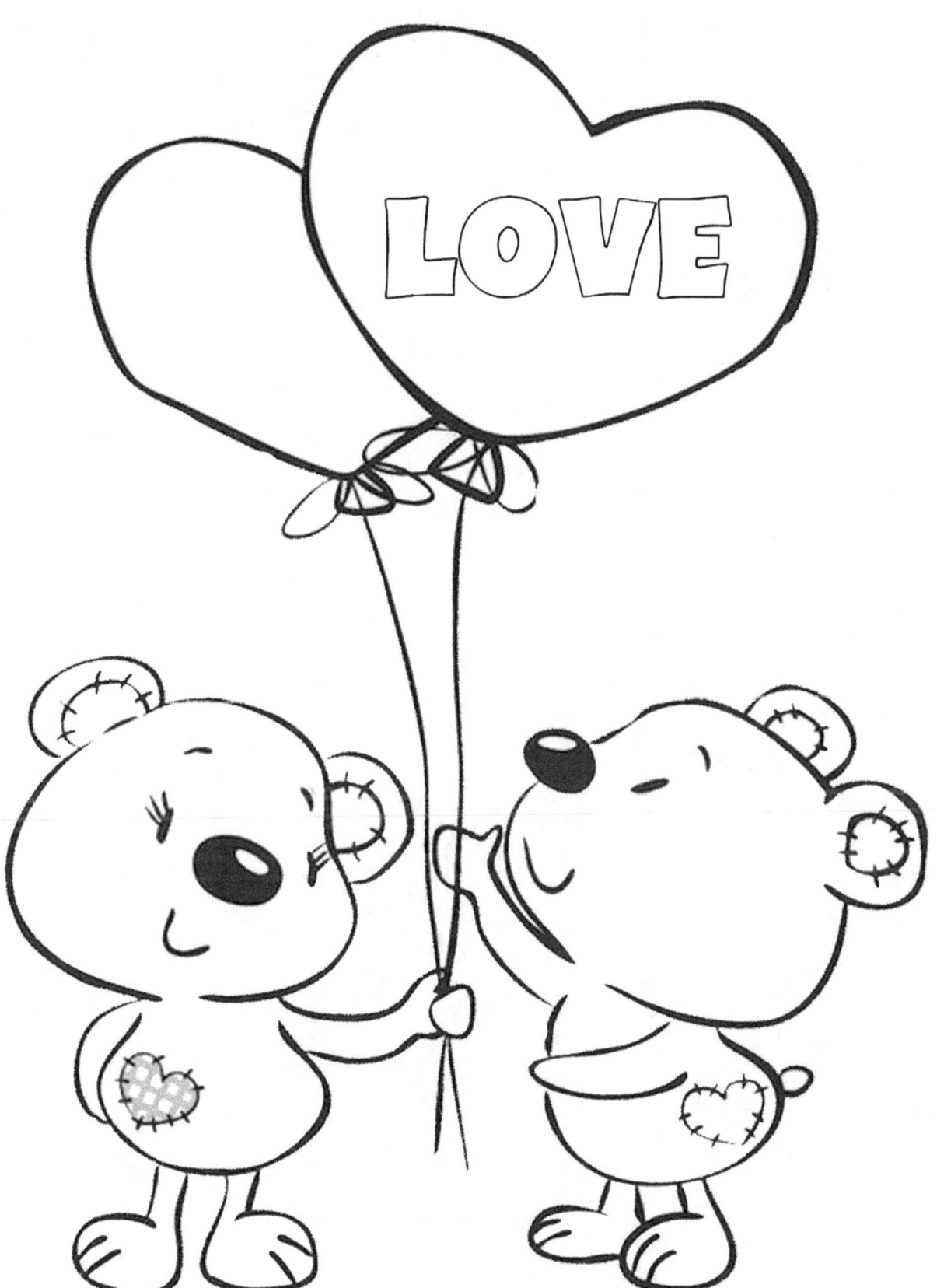

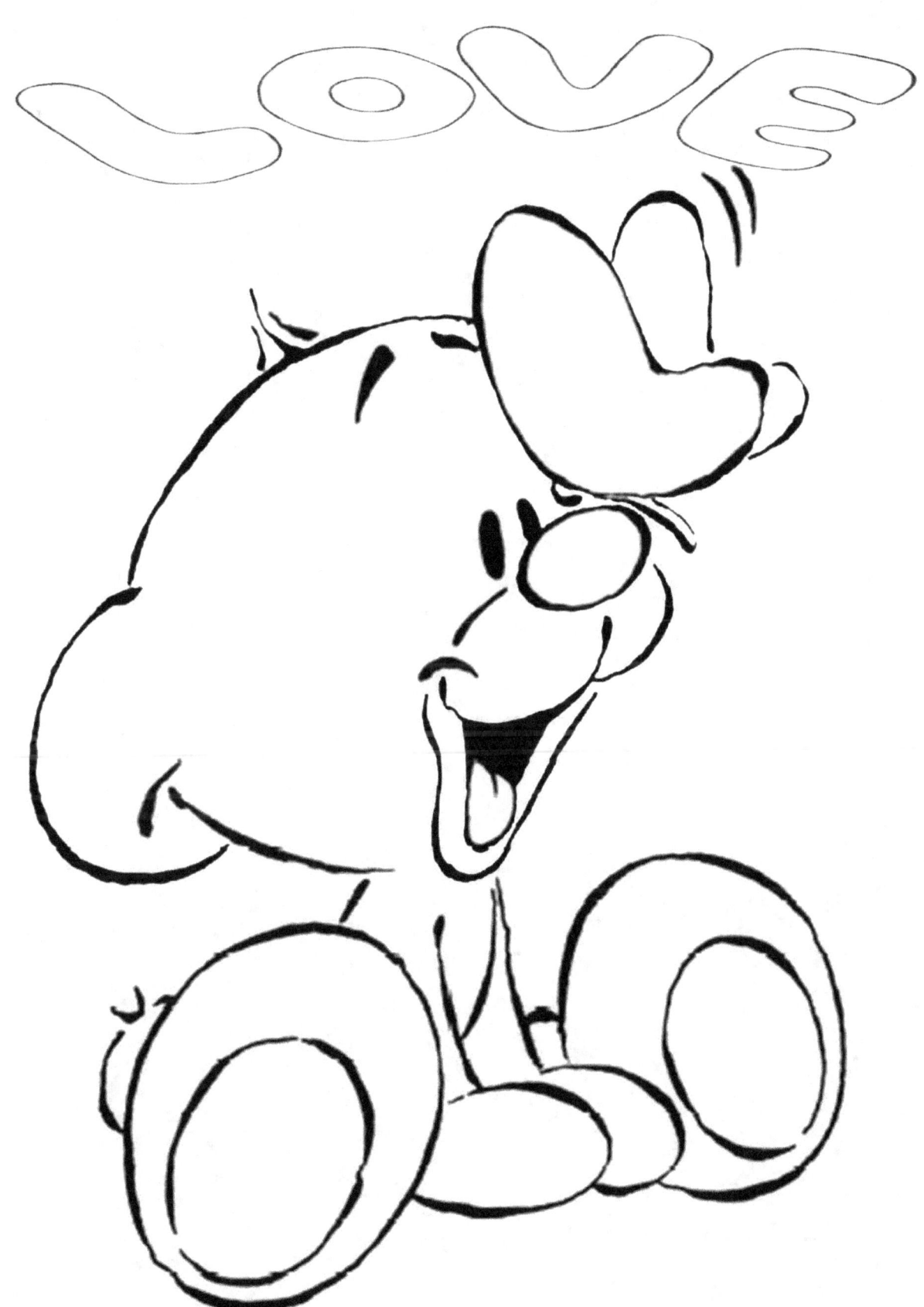

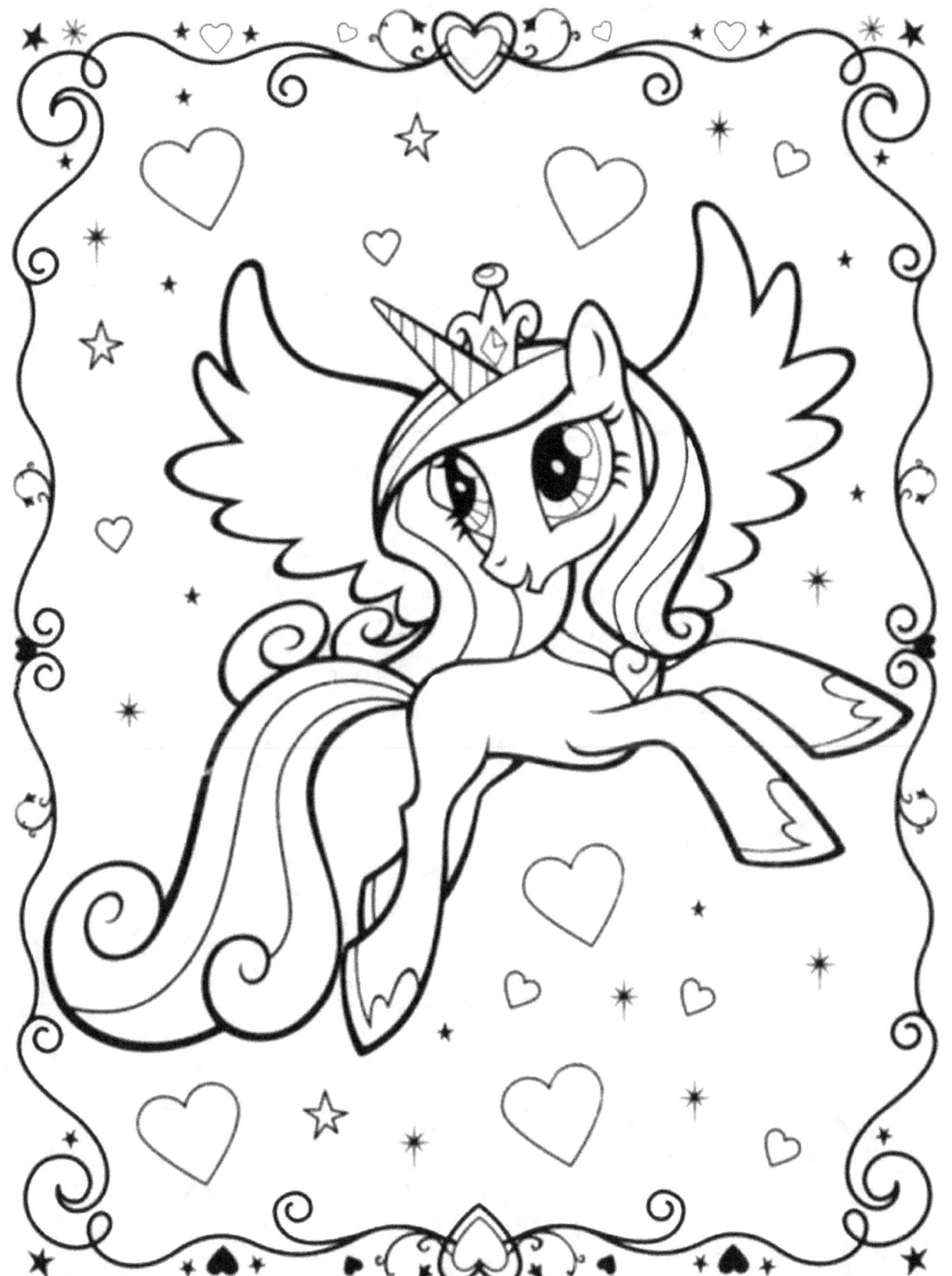

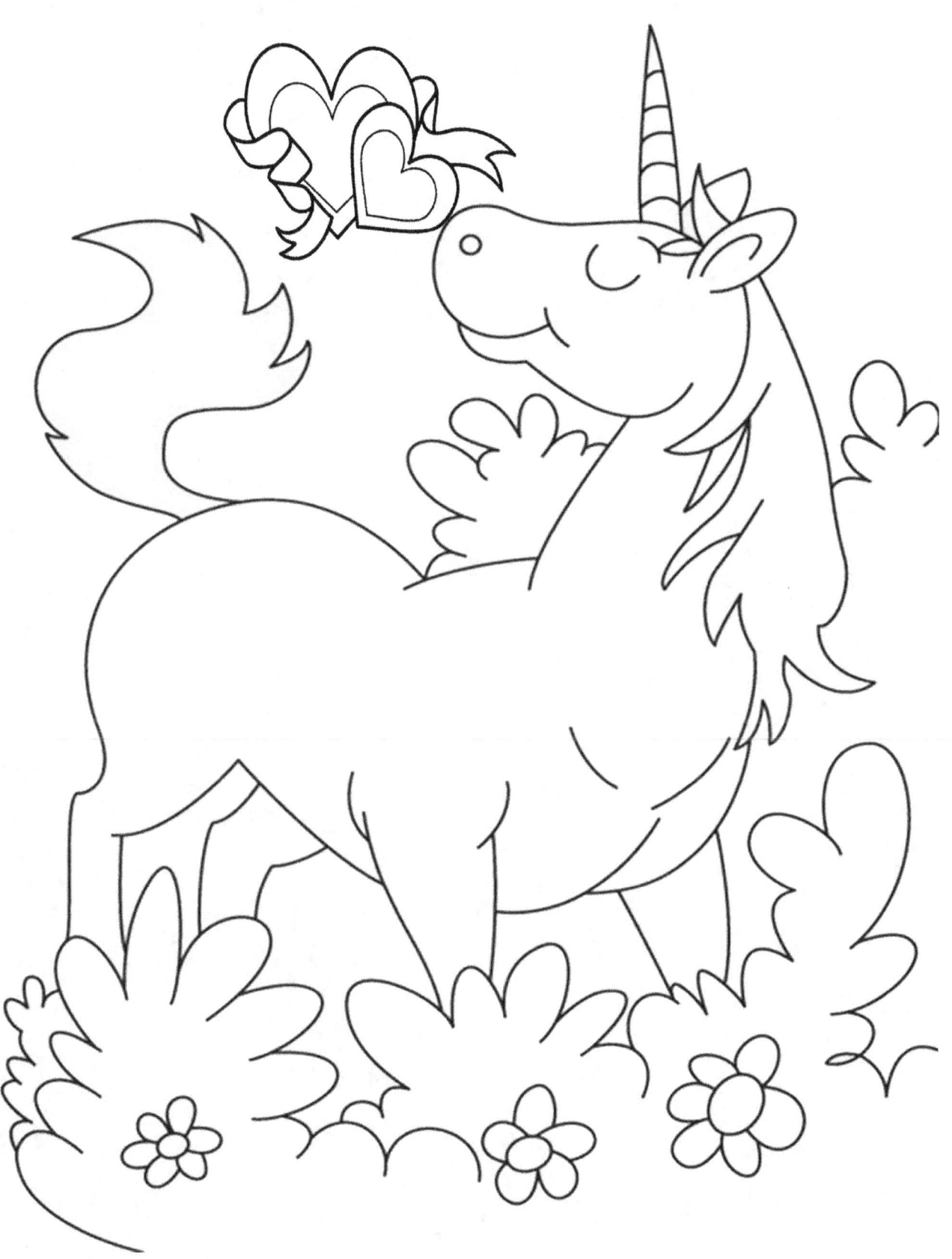

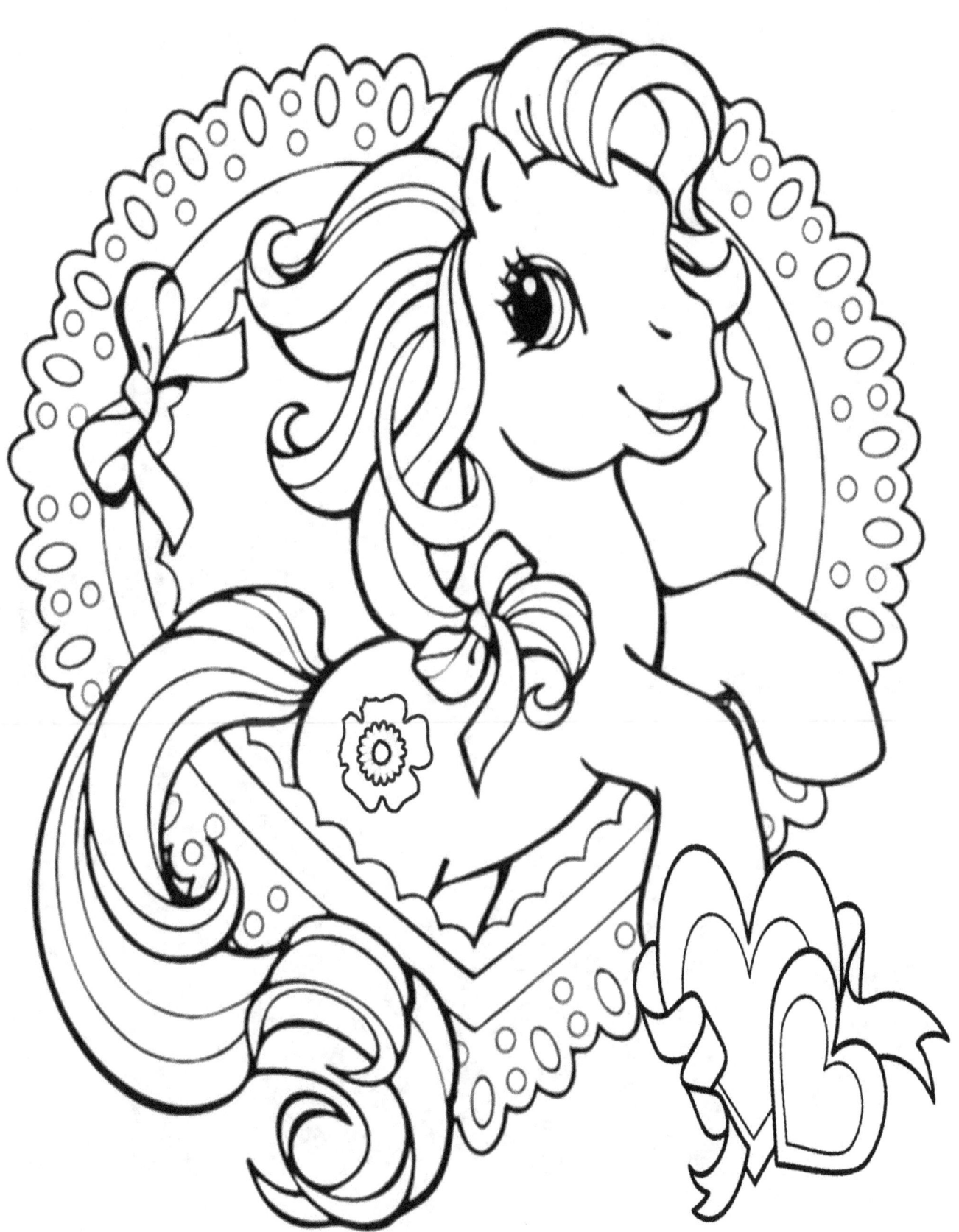

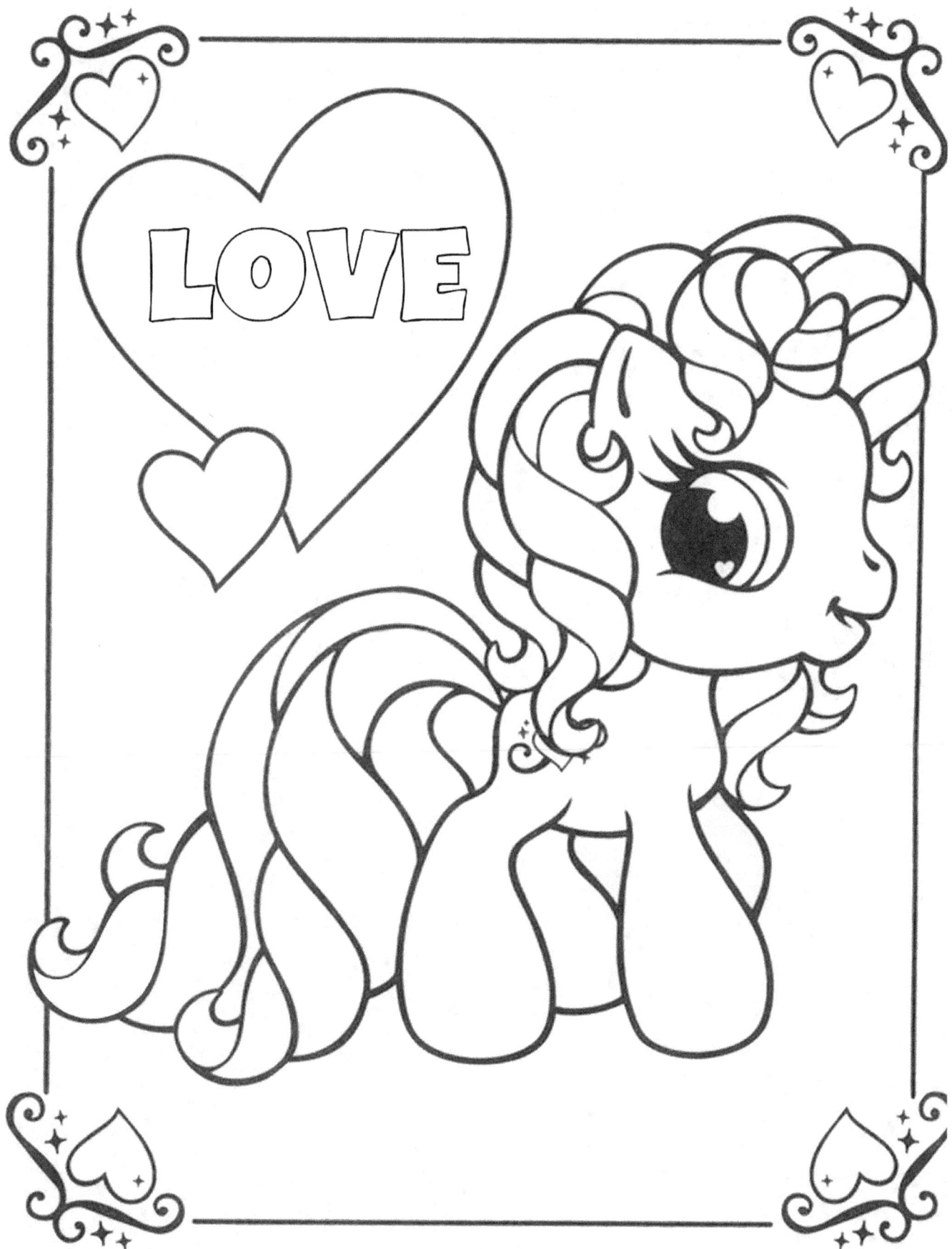

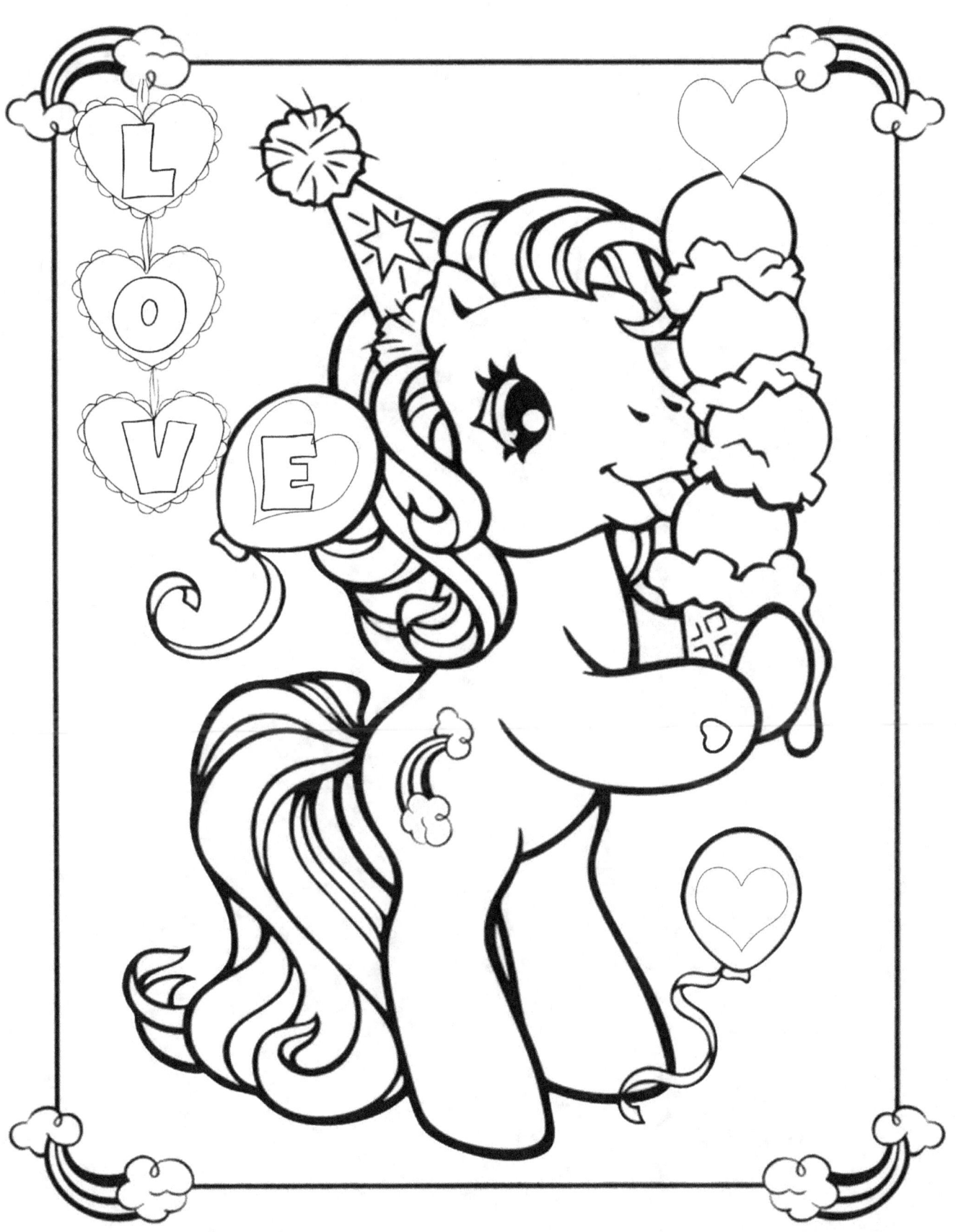

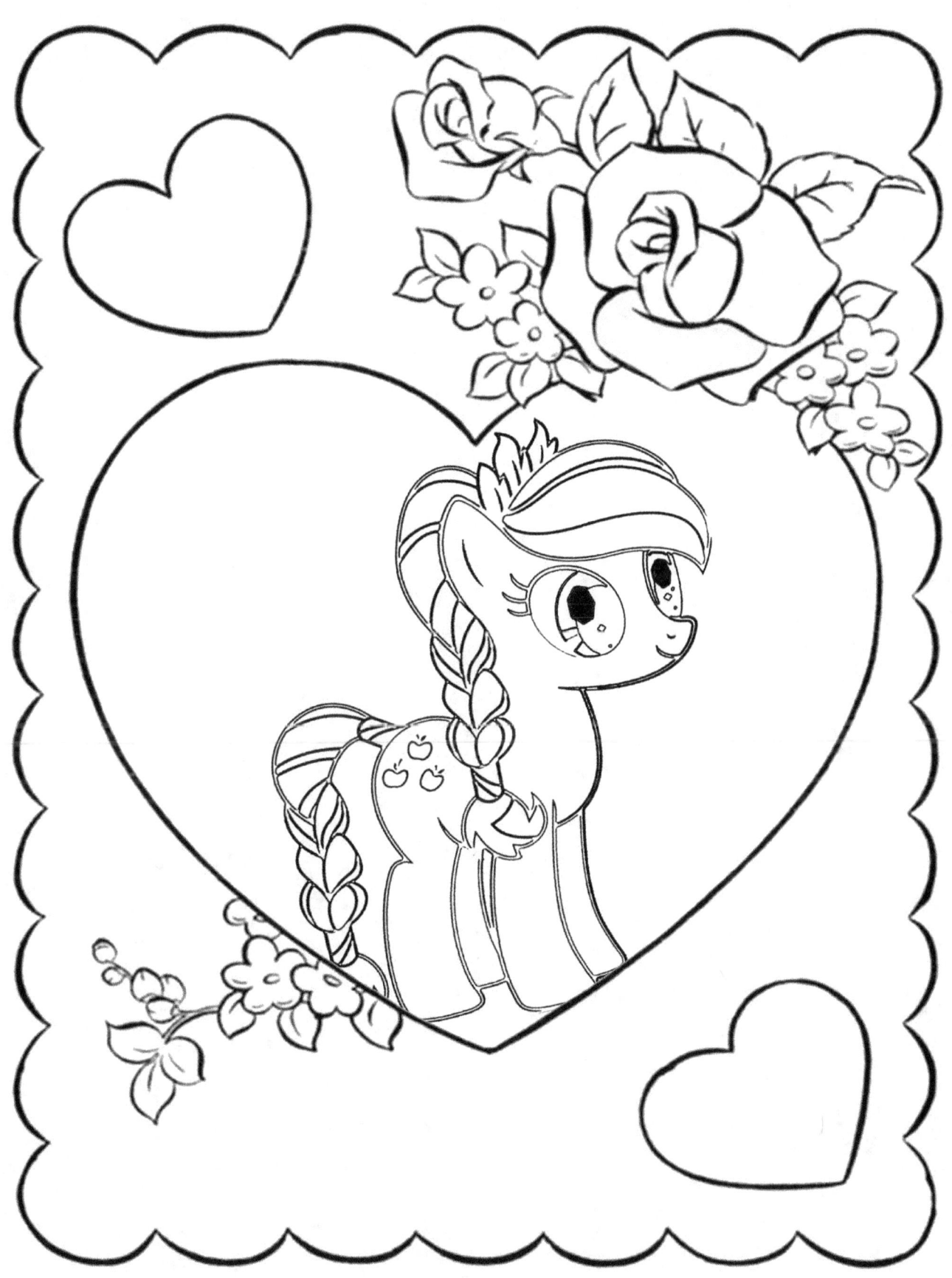

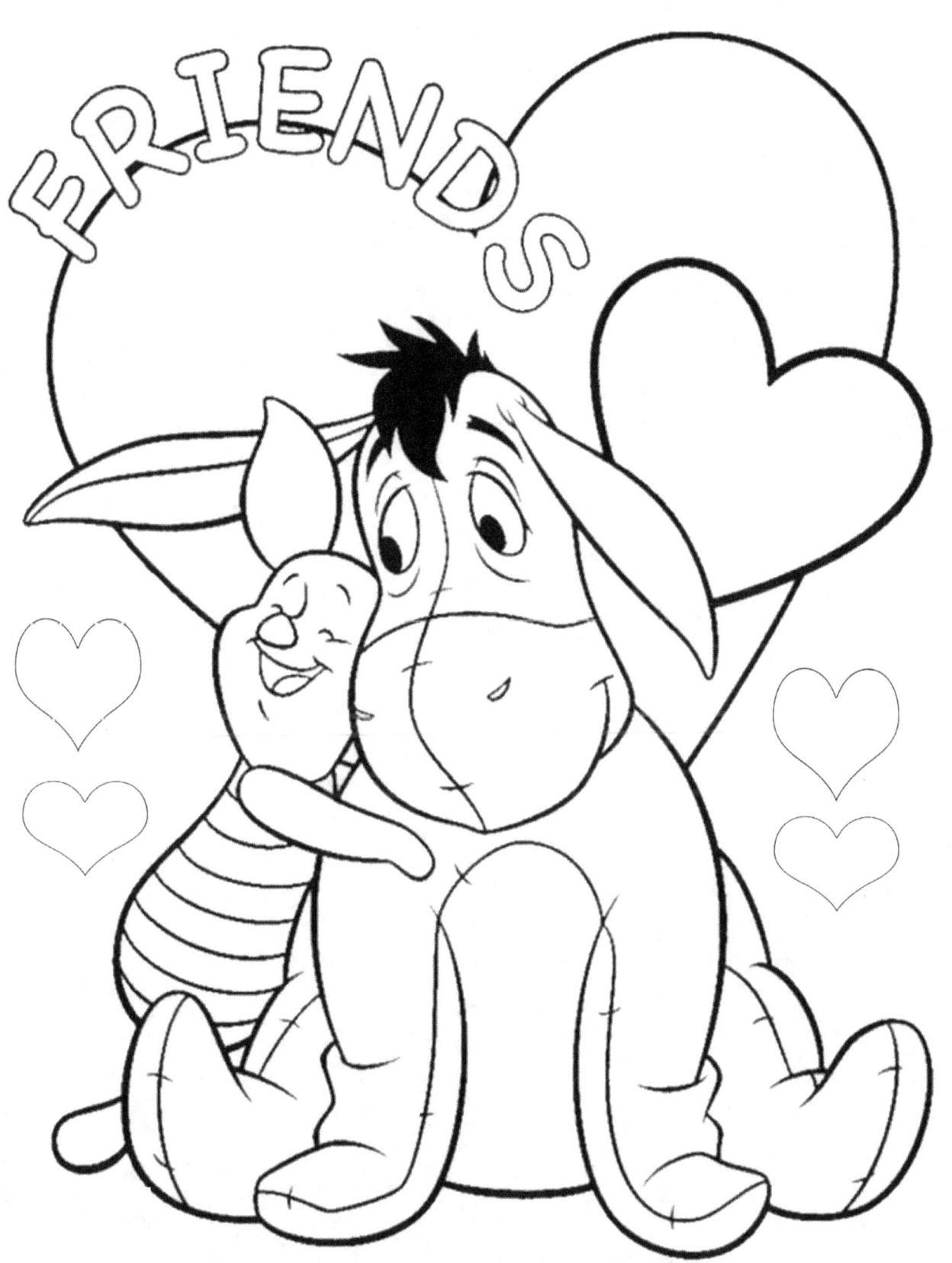

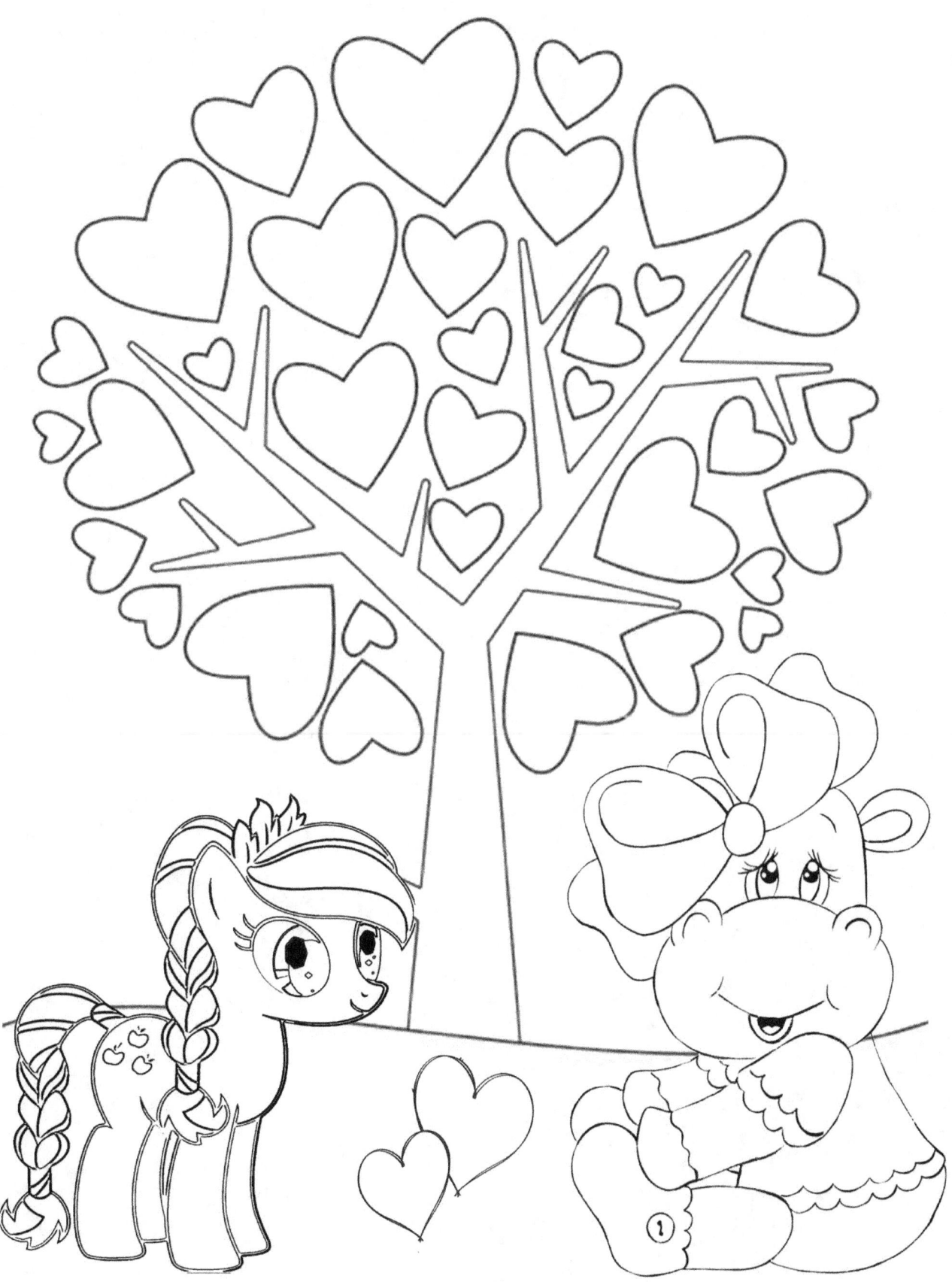

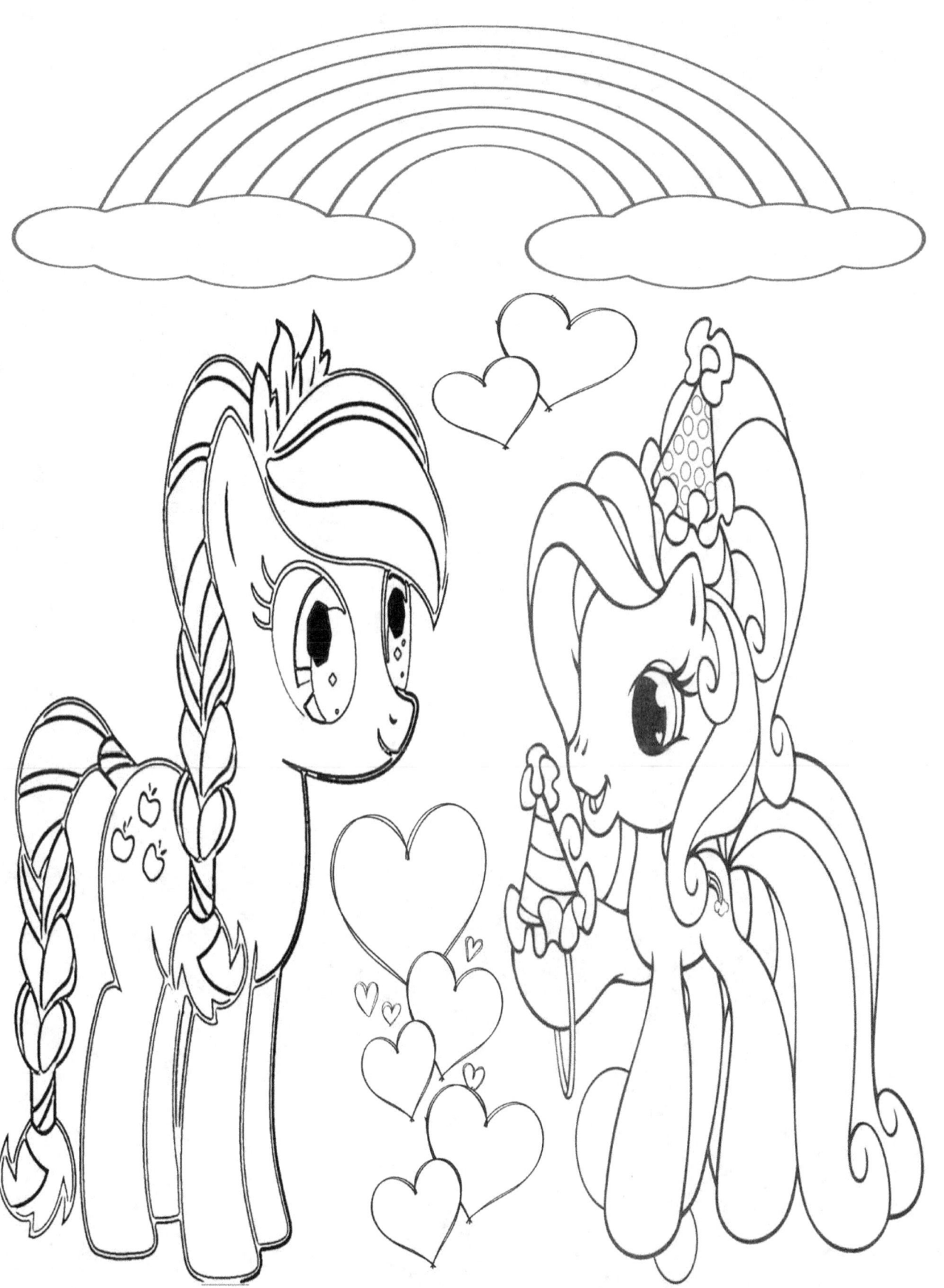

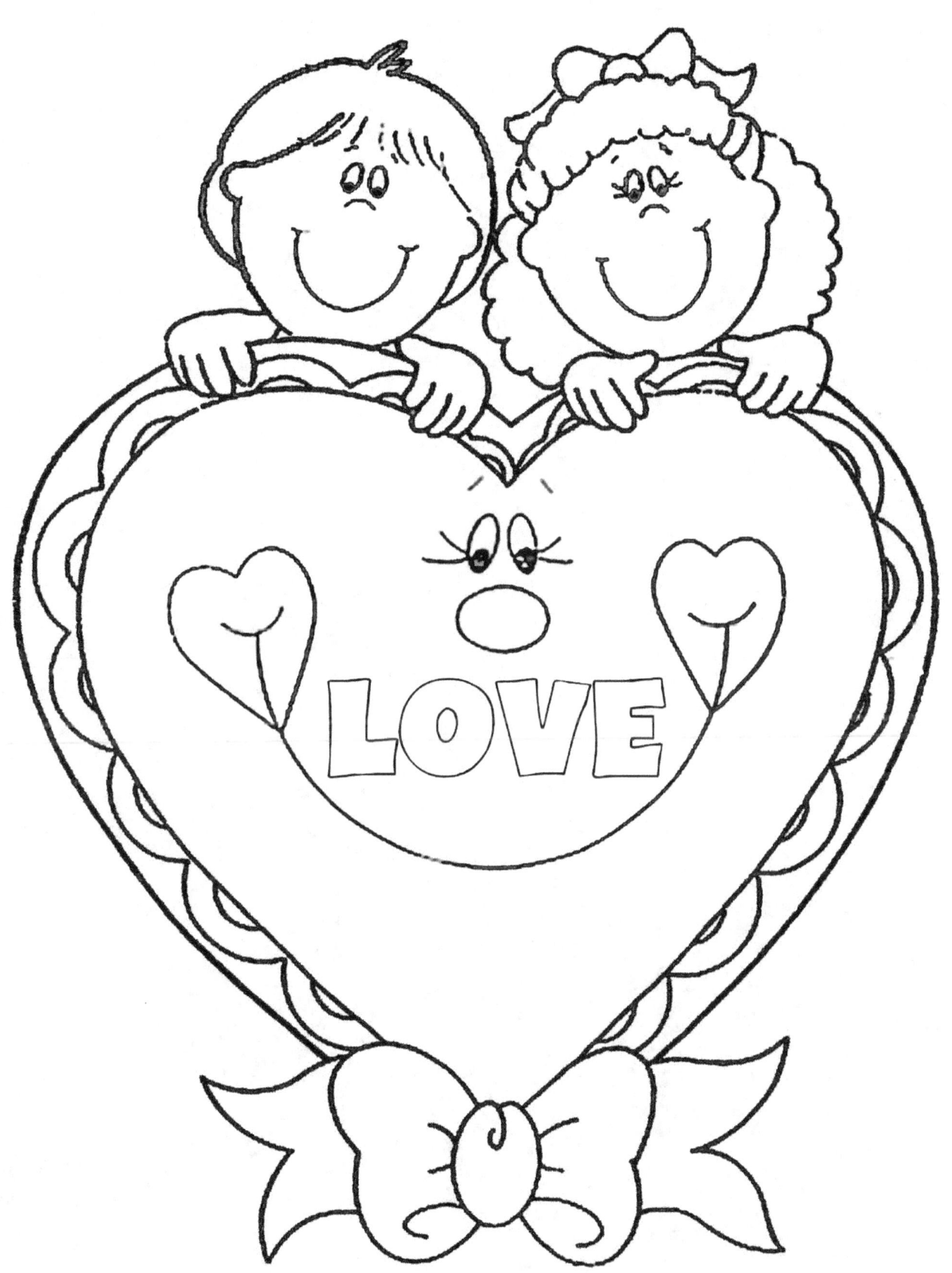

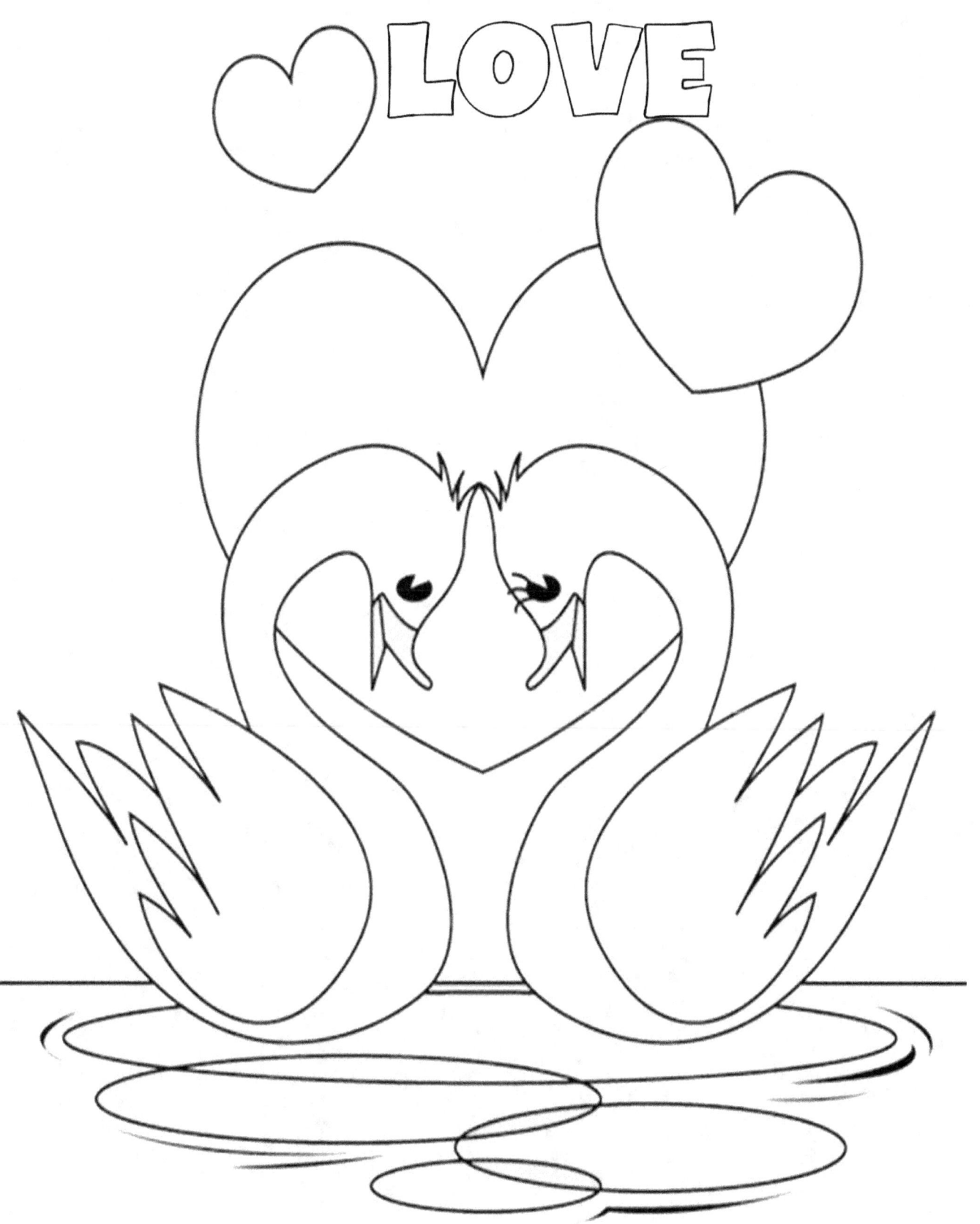

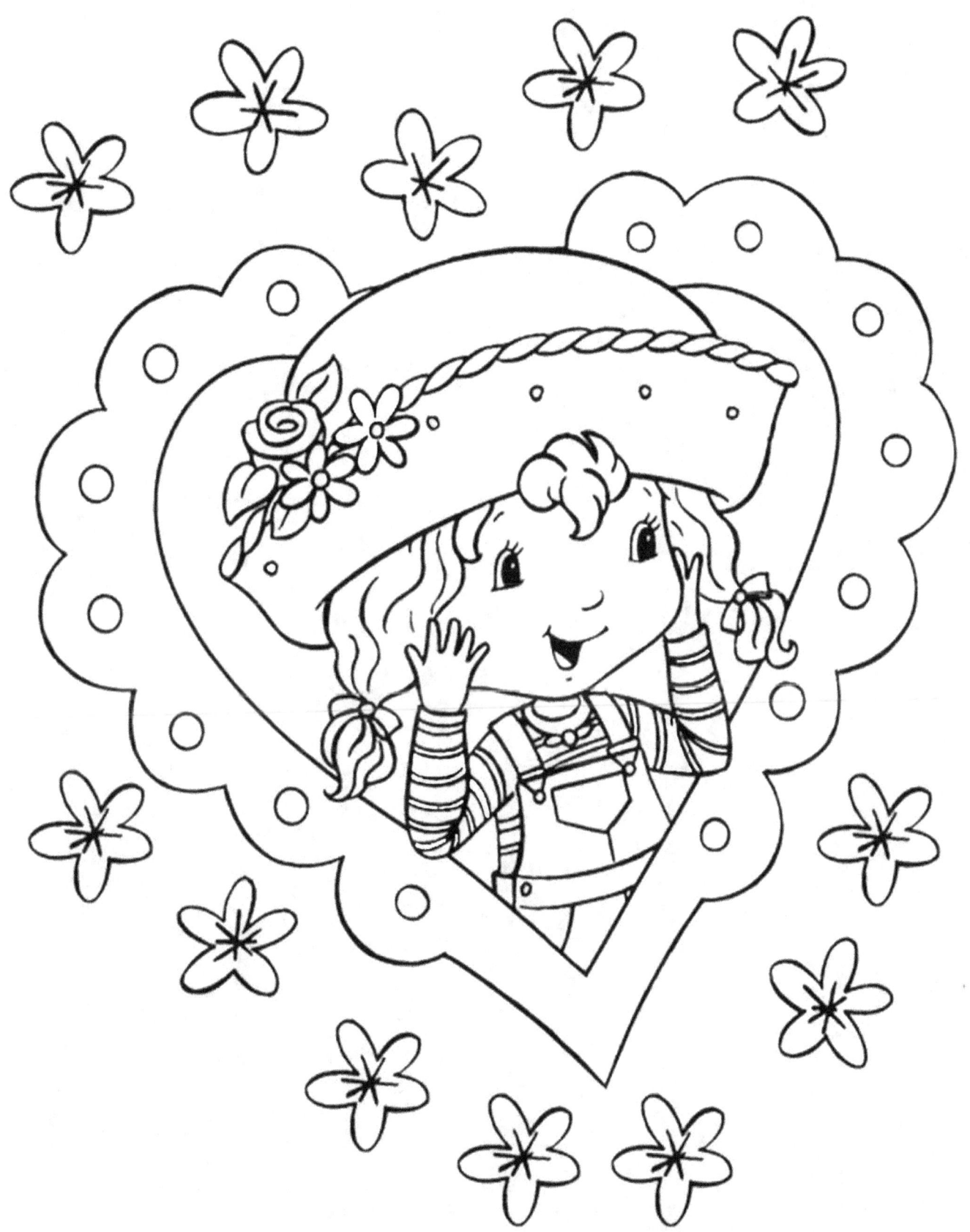

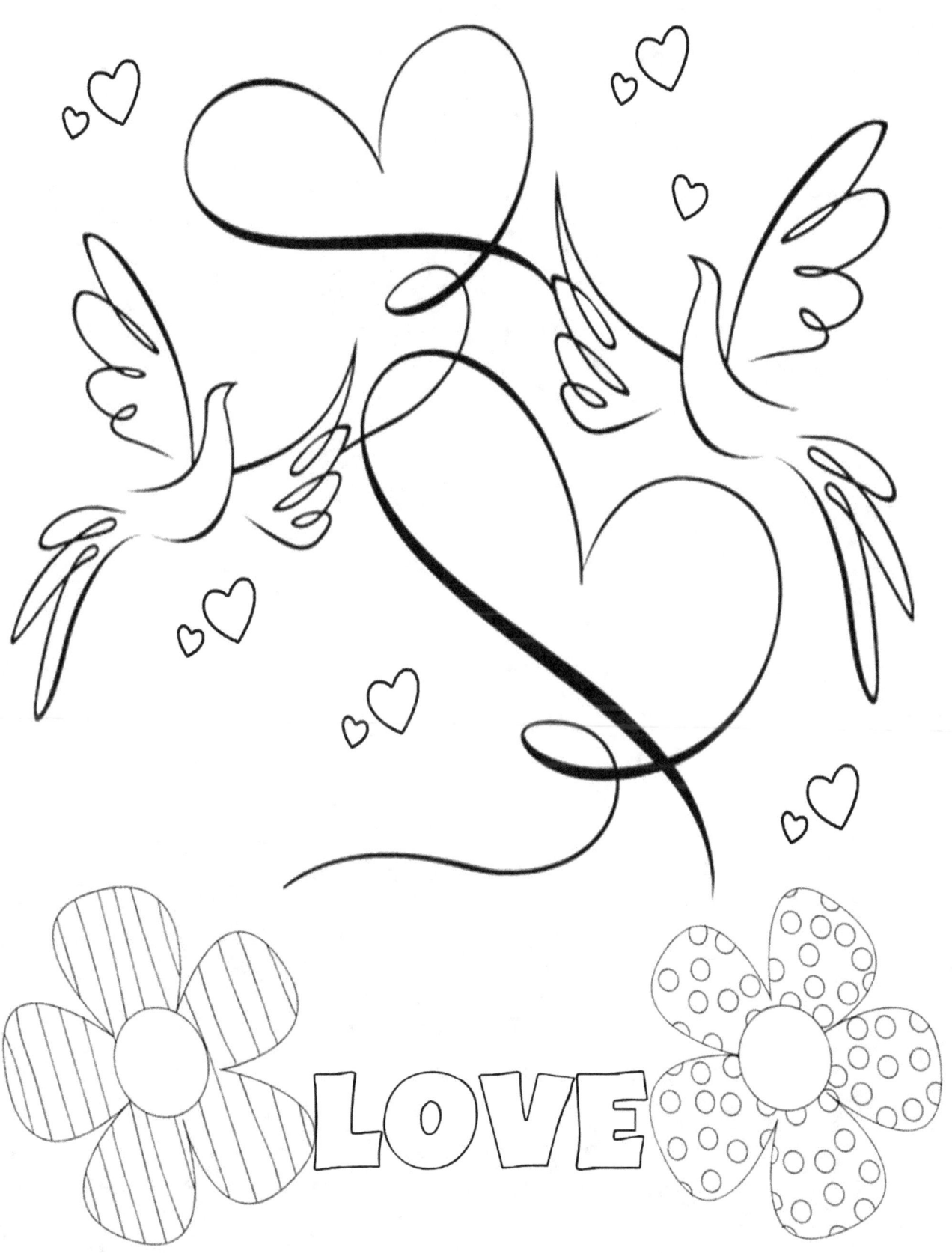

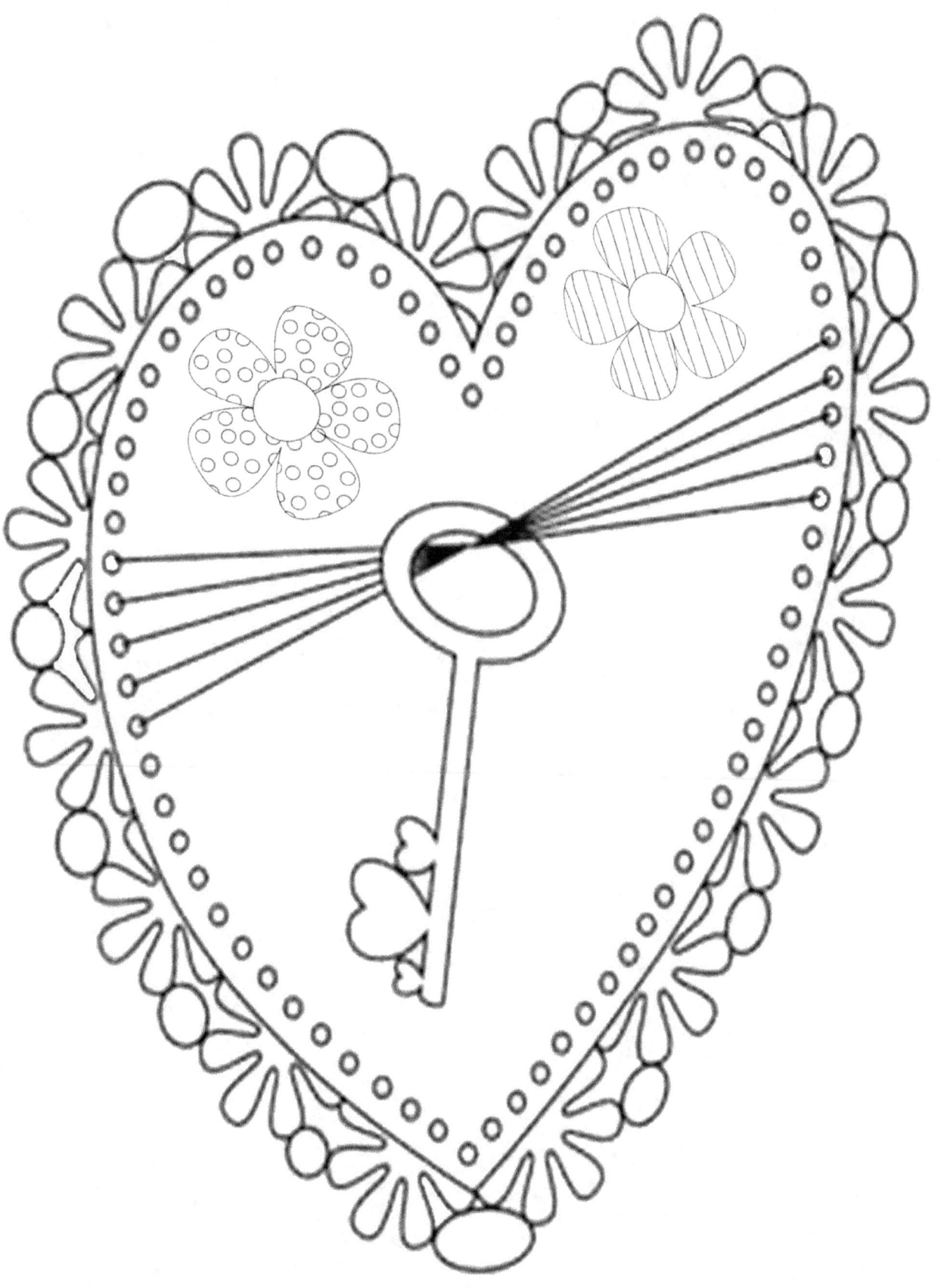

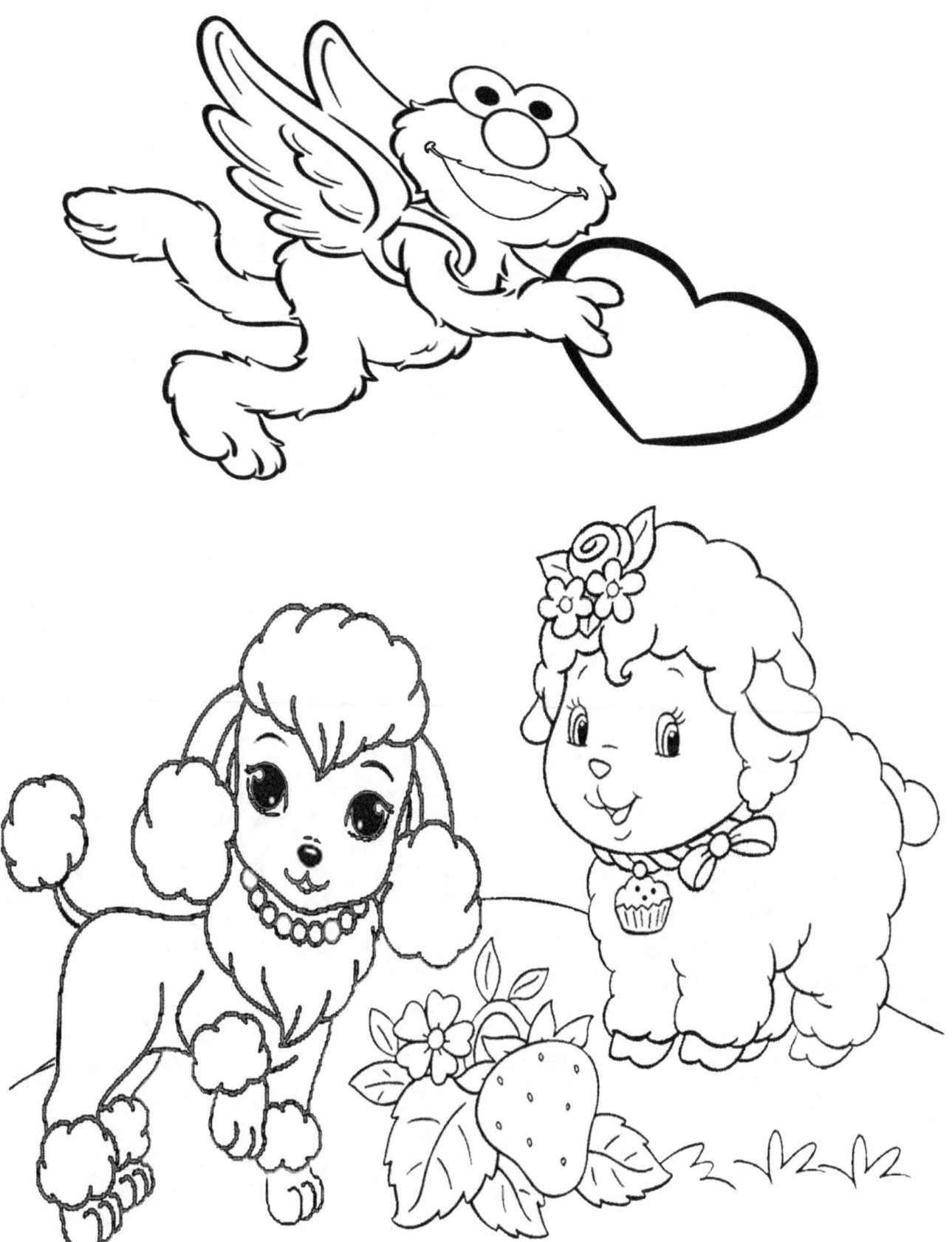

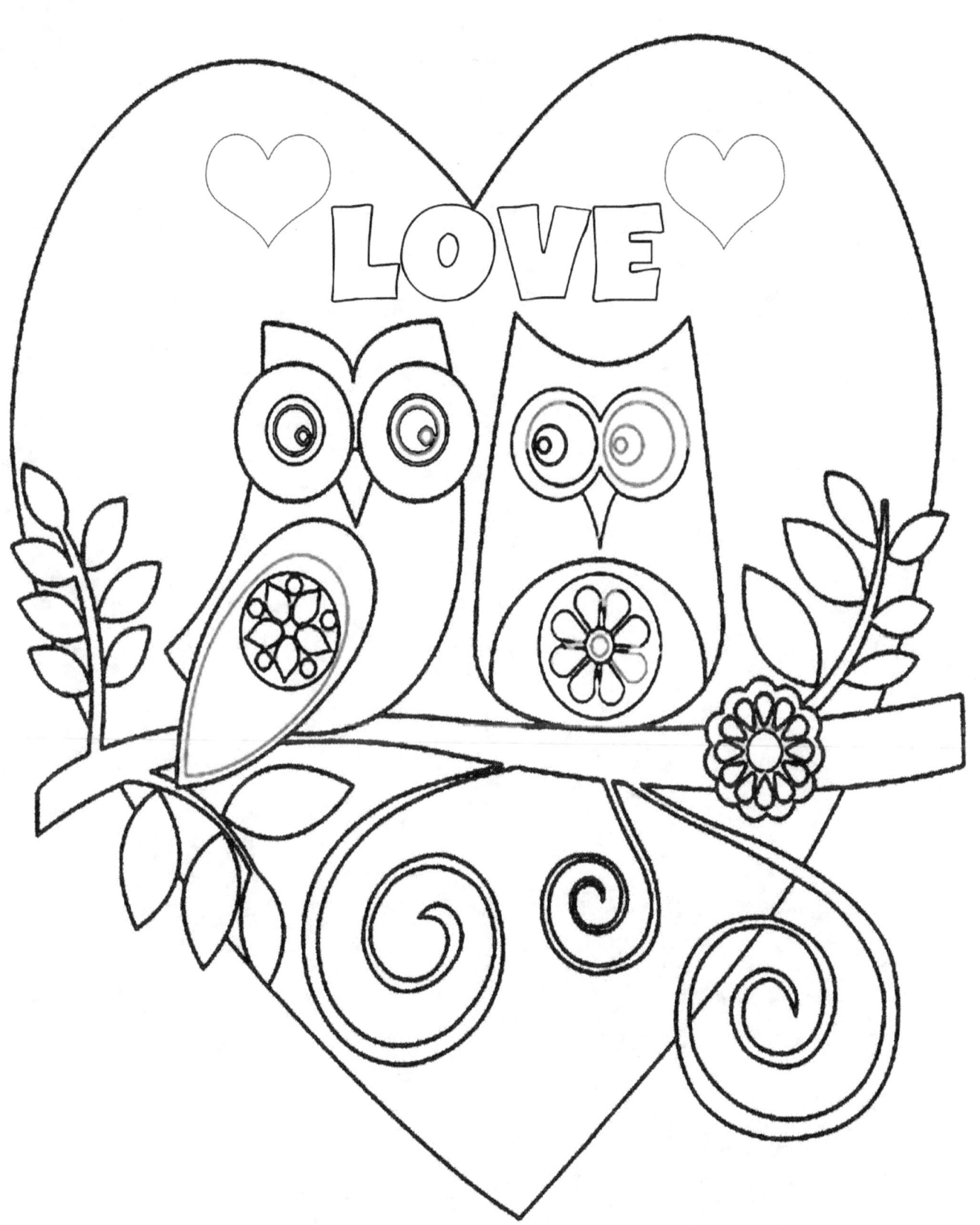

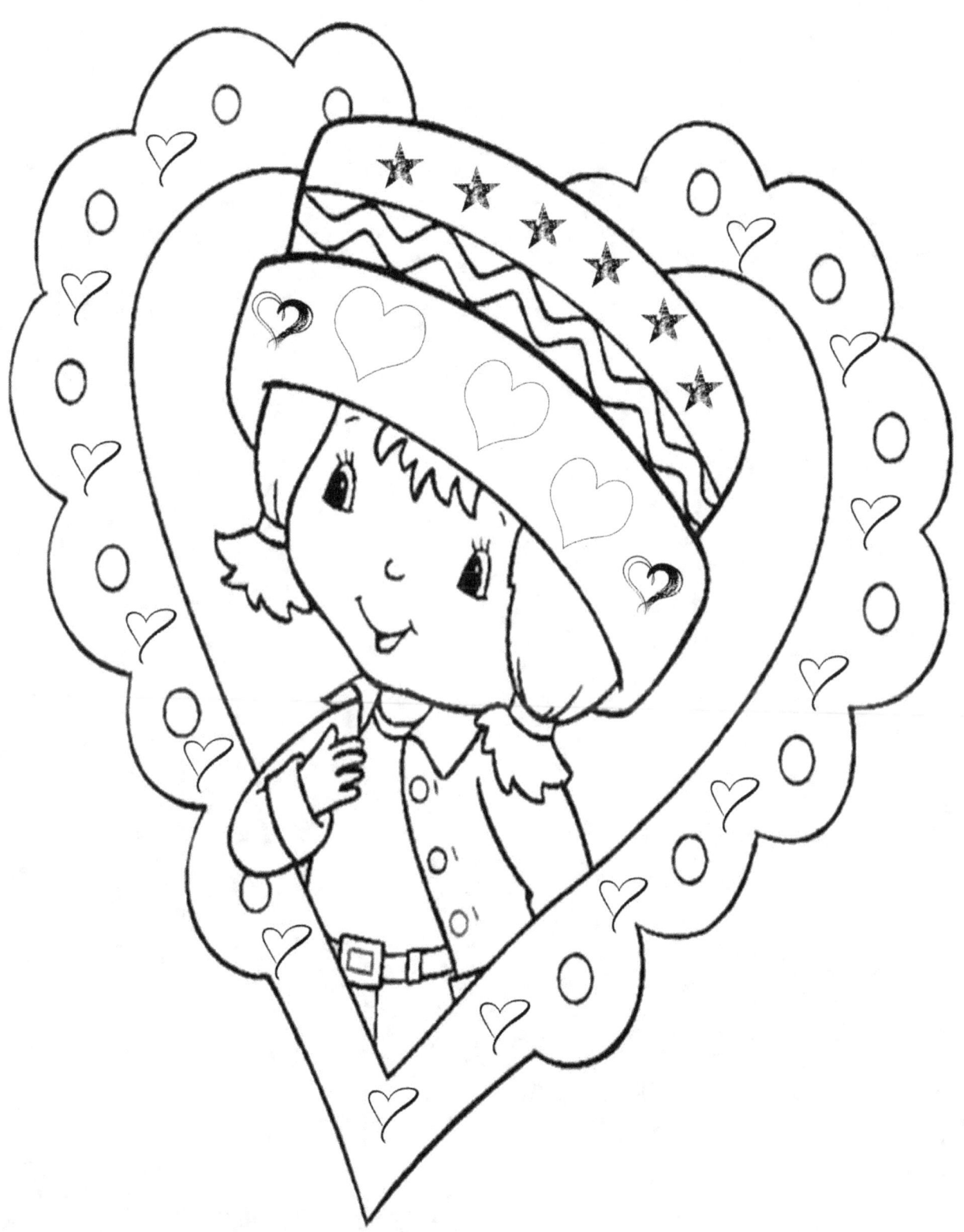

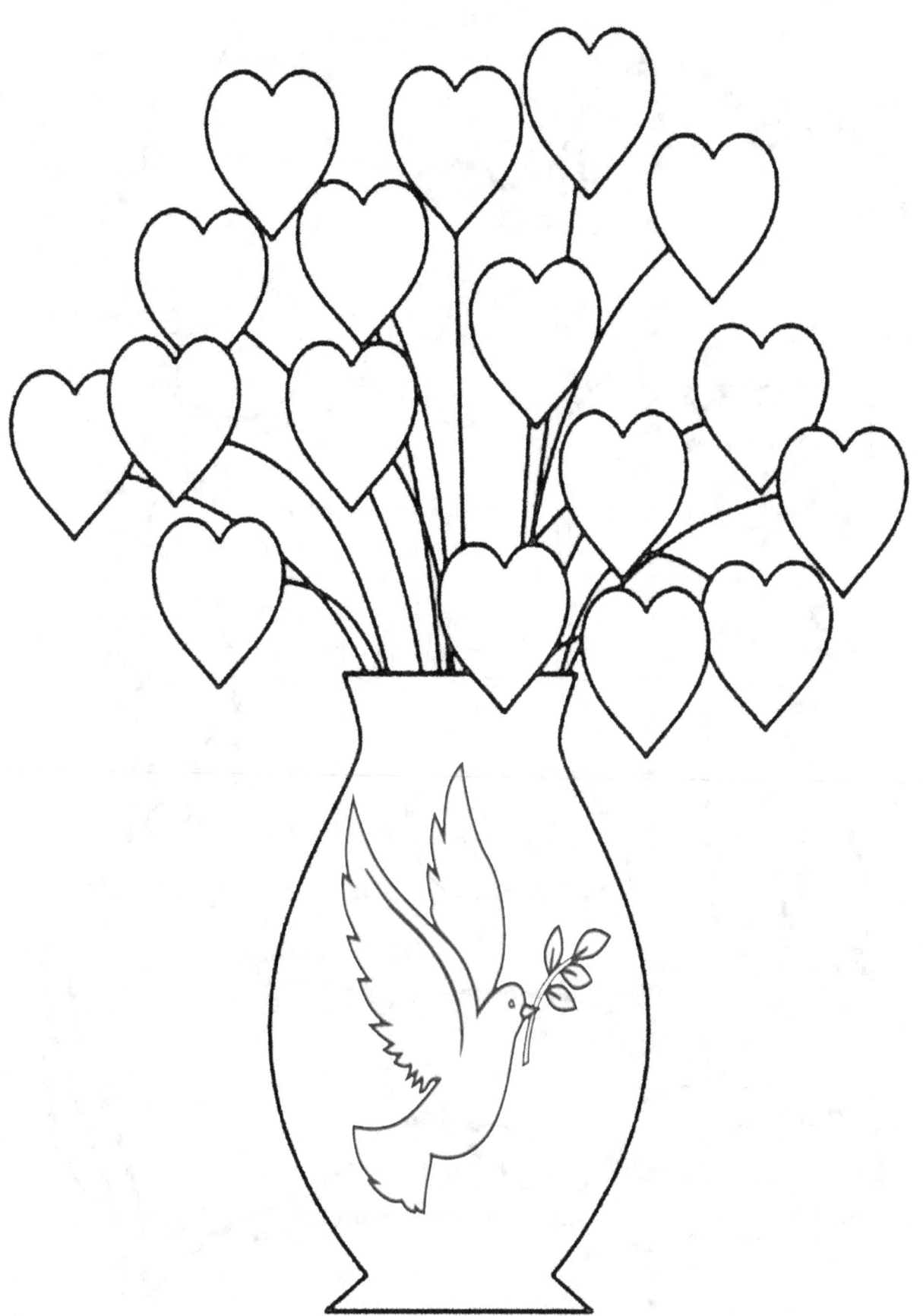

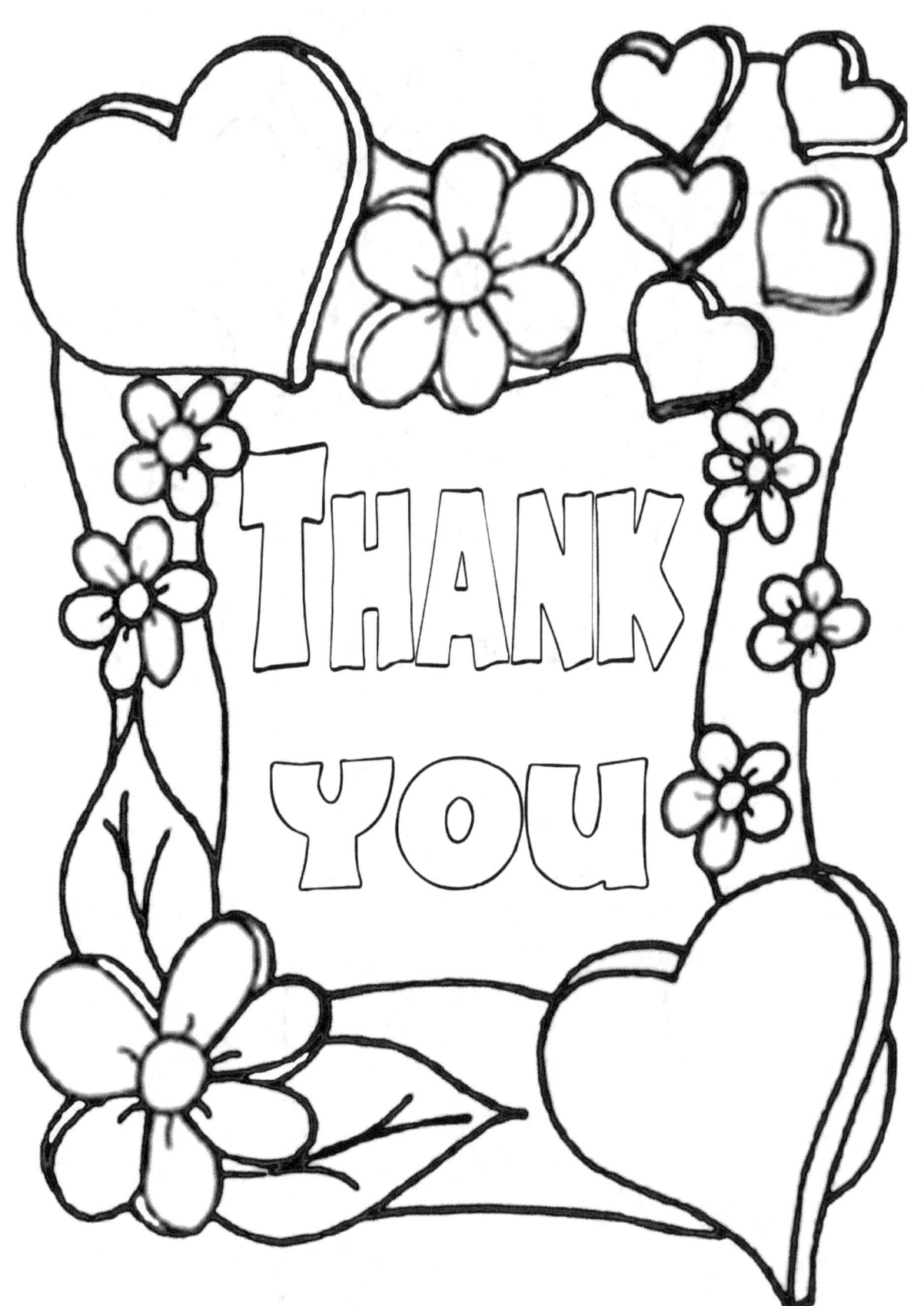